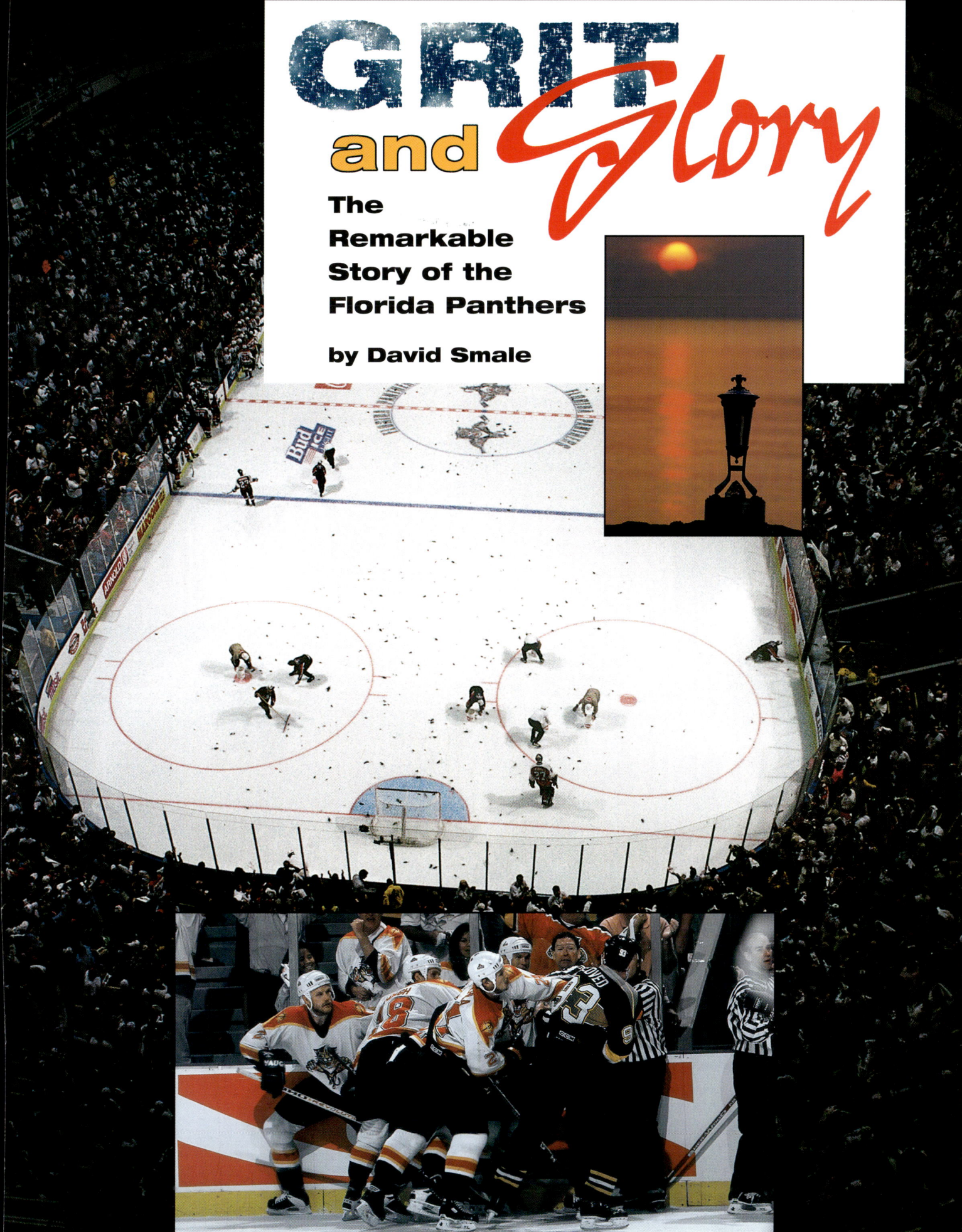

GRIT and Glory

The Remarkable Story of the Florida Panthers

by David Smale

Dedication

To my own Stanley Cup champions:
Tammy, David Lee and Julie

All photographs courtesy of:
The Florida Panthers
Ken Denardo

Rainbow Publishing
4750 Belinder Road
Westwood, Kansas 66205
(913) 384-5899

Rainbow Publishing
David Smale, Vice President, Managing Editor,
Project Coordinator
Ray Smale, Vice President, Chief Financial Officer
Geof Payne, Designer

Printed in the U.S.A.
by
Jostens Printing and Publishing
ISBN 0-9648680-4-0

CONTENTS

GRIT and Glory

The Remarkable Story of the Florida Panthers

by David Smale

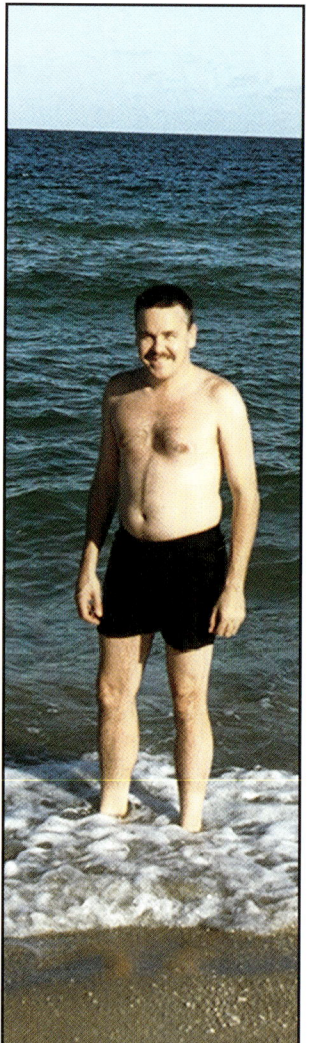

I got on an airplane early one morning last October. I was leaving Kansas City to head to South Florida to write a book on a hockey team. As my plane took off, the rain was changing to freezing rain with the possibility of snow later in the day. Significant snowfall in October is very rare in Kansas City, so I wasn't too concerned that my family would have trouble while I was gone.

It didn't take long for me to figure out that this was one great story.

When I got off the plane in Fort Lauderdale, the temperature was in the 80s with a light breeze. I got my luggage, rented a car, checked into the hotel and went to the Panthers offices to meet the people with whom I would be spending the next 10 days. In the back of my mind, I wondered what the weather was like back home. When I finally returned to the hotel and called home, I found out that the freezing rain had changed to snow and by 5 p.m. Central time, there was 8 inches of the white stuff on the ground. There was ice mixed in, causing tree branches to break, many of which fell on power lines causing massive power outages. I was sweating, having hurried around in the South Florida heat and humidity, but my family was shivering without power. The cold snap lasted a week, and our neighborhood looked like a war zone. When I finally returned home on October 31st, it was seasonably warm once again (mid-70s), but my tan let people know I hadn't been spending my time the same way they had over the past 10 days.

As strange as the climactic differences sounded, it wasn't any stranger than what I was in South Florida to do. A hockey team in South Florida? It has been said the only ice that South Floridians know about is the crushed ice in their drinks. Yet, not only was there a team that played its games in Miami, but it was a darned good one. And it also was one of the "hottest" teams on ice, in terms of fan support.

It didn't take long for me to figure out that this was one great story. My second night in town I attended a Panthers game at Miami Arena against the

Ottawa Senators. The Panthers won, 5-2, the eighth straight game without a loss to start the season. The streak reached 12 before the Philadelphia Flyers finally stopped it. The enthusiasm in the arena was deafening—and inspirational, I'm sure, to the team. After the game, I saw the players mingling with the fans, not in some prearranged "Get to Know Your Team" show, but just like two friends getting together after work.

I went to practice the next day and got to know the players myself. Greg Bouris, then the team's director of public relations, tabbed them "The Franchise You Can Touch," and I found that to be true. I have covered college and professional sports for most of my adult life, but rarely had I found a group of athletes so approachable and so cooperative. To the team, I say thanks for making my job easier.

Greg and I became fast friends. Maybe part of it was the fact that he had worked for the New York Islanders and I had lived on Long Island during their heyday. Maybe it was the fact that we both are sports fans. Either way, we hit it off and I enjoyed his company. He was very helpful in my research for this book, so you should join me in saying thanks to Greg for all his help.

Other members of the Panthers front office were helpful, too. Ron Dennis, the director of merchandising, was an enthusiastic supporter of this project from the very beginning. A fellow Promise Keeper, Ron invited me to his church the Sunday I was in South Florida, so I didn't feel alone. Thanks Ron.

Everyone from Wayne Huizenga, Bill Torrey, Bryan Murray and Doug MacLean to the administrative assistants to the clubhouse staff greeted me warmly and granted any requests I had. It is so much easier to write a book when the organization is behind it.

Hockey is a great sport. You knew that. The Florida Panthers are an exciting team to watch. You knew that, too. But more than that, the Florida Panthers organization is made up of people who care: about their team, about hockey and about each other. In this era of self-centeredness and "looking out for number one," it is refreshing to find an organization that does things the right way.

The Panthers history is a short one, but it already is a full one. I consider myself a big Panthers fan, and I wear my Panthers shirts proudly. How privileged I was to be the one to write this story. I thank you for letting me into your lives. I hope you have as much fun reading and reminiscing as I did writing it. If you do, then I did my job.

God Bless you.

David

David Smale

 While the author's family was "enjoying" an early 8-inch snowstorm in the midwest, he was discovering some of the benefits of covering a hockey team in South Florida.

The Florida Panthers reached respectability immediately. They nearly reached the playoffs in their first season. By the end of their third season of existence, the *Felis Concolor Coryi* had reached the Stanley Cup Finals. It should come as no surprise, therefore, to know that relatively speaking, the Panthers franchise became a reality in a matter of minutes.

Four weeks after H. Wayne Huizenga first met Bruce McNall, then owner of the Los Angeles Kings and chairman of the National Hockey League's Board of Governors, South Florida had a hockey team. Huizenga, who grew up in Chicago where he attended "a couple of games," was not a hockey fan. But he was a hockey owner.

Huizenga went to southern California in November 1992 for a meeting with Michael Eisner, chairman of the Disney Company. As chairman of Blockbuster Entertainment Corporation, Huizenga was becoming a major player in the entertainment business, and he and Eisner had deals to discuss. After the meeting, Huizenga went back to the airport. Huizenga also owned the Florida Marlins, the major league baseball team that would begin operations in the National League the next spring, and he was in the market for a plane to tote the team.

His pilot told him that there was a 727 for sale, and he could use this opportunity to look at it. The plane was owned by McNall, who walked onto the plane while Huizenga was getting his tour. "That was the first time I had ever met him," Huizenga said. "We said hello and exchanged small talk. I asked him, 'Are you guys thinking about putting a team in Florida?'

"They had just attempted to get a team in South Florida. The person they chose did not get awarded a franchise. The franchises went to Tampa and Ottawa. He asked if I was interested in owning a team. I had said back in those days that I had no interest in a team myself, but for the good of South Florida, I would step up and try to help someone who wanted to bring it here. I just never anticipated that I would be the one who brought hockey here."

Apparently, McNall saw something in Huizenga, because he persisted. He told Huizenga that if he became interested, he should call Gil Stein, the Interim President of the NHL. Maybe more importantly, he also called Stein and told him about Huizenga.

Huizenga's name quickly was becoming familiar in sports circles. Besides owning the expansion Marlins, he had purchased 15 percent of the Miami Dolphins and 50 percent of Joe Robbie Stadium (the home of the Dolphins). He currently owns 100 percent of the team and the stadium, now called Pro Player Stadium.

A week after his encounter with McNall, Huizenga received a call from Stein, who related that he had heard of the meeting. "He said, 'Next time you're in New York, how about stopping by?'" Huizenga said. "I looked at my calendar and told him I would be in New York a month later, and we set up a meeting. I figured it was the beginning of a two- or three-year deal."

Before there was time

When Gary Bettman and the NHL awarded a franchise to Wayne Huizenga and South Florida, it made the area one of a few regions in the country to have franchises in all four major professional sports. But there was no time to celebrate as the season started in 10 months.

Huizenga made his trip to New York and dropped by the league office. Stein told him that there was a possibility of the league expanding much sooner than anyone anticipated. "He said they had some very unusual circumstances," Huizenga said. "I didn't know it then, but he was talking about Disney. It's interesting that when I met McNall, I had just come from Disney's office."

The NHL was interested in Huizenga, partly because of his ownership of Blockbuster. With Disney involved, if the league could convince Blockbuster to join, "it would show the public that big companies are interested in the NHL," Huizenga said.

Huizenga would not commit Blockbuster to owning a team in South Florida when he wasn't positive it would be a success. "That wasn't our main business," he said. But he was ready to commit himself to it. And he didn't get where he is in business by throwing his money away.

Huizenga was confident that the area could support a hockey team. What could be more traditional than coming out after attending a hockey game, getting into your convertible and heading home to your beach house? Huh? "Most of the people who live here are from the north," he said. "On the west coast of Florida, you have people from the midwest. On this coast, you have all the northeast people. And northeast people know hockey. Plus we have a lot of Canadians."

At the conclusion of the meeting with Huizenga, Stein told Huizenga that he would talk to some of the other owners and would be in touch. The next conversation was Stein calling Huizenga to tell him it was up to him.

The NHL was interested in Huizenga, partly because of his ownership of Blockbuster.

"We didn't have time to do any surveys or anything like that," Huizenga said. "It was one of those on-the-spot, do-you-want-it-or-don't-you type of things. So I said yes. I figured we could bring in some partners."

Huizenga still didn't know who the other prospective owner was. Stein's only clue was that it was a company from the west coast. During one conversation, Stein let it slip that it was a company in California, a state with franchises in the San Francisco area (San Jose Sharks) and in Los Angeles (Kings). That left San Diego as the only major market in the state without a franchise.

"I tried to pin him down," Huizenga said. "He said, 'We've got a 25-mile limit, but we're going to get a waiver.'"

The final hurdle for getting a franchise was approval of the other owners at the league meeting, held, ironically, in Palm Beach, Florida. Stein called Huizenga and invited him to attend the meeting. "He said, 'Let's get together in my suite. If we can get this thing put through, I'll come up to the suite and get you and bring you back down to introduce you to the owners. Michael will be there too.' That was the first clue I had that it was Michael Eisner and Disney. I called Michael and he confirmed it."

Huizenga believes that it was Disney-driven—the league wanted Disney in the league and needed a second franchise. But Huizenga's aggressive style would be welcomed. On December 10, 1992, the Board of Governors voted to award franchises to Huizenga and Disney. About a month after the initial discussion, Huizenga had a hat trick—ownership of franchises in three major professional sports leagues.

There were a few major differences in the way South Florida got a hockey team and the normal route. Most communities will put together a package of ownership, facilities, marketing plans and an already-established season-ticket base. The process takes months, maybe years, before a league acquiesces and awards the franchise.

This took days, and Huizenga was on his own. He didn't have a facility or a marketing

plan. He didn't have a ticket base; he didn't even have a way to take orders for tickets. The switchboard at Blockbuster's headquarters lit up like a Christmas tree the day after the announcement. Fans flooded the phones with calls regarding tickets. There were so many calls that Blockbuster had to call in extra help to answer the phones.

With the franchise awarded, there still were a few questions left to answer: Who? What? When? Where? Why? And how? Some were easy to answer. What? To assemble a hockey organization and team. Why? The proverbial answer: because it (the franchise) is there. How? With Wayne Huizenga in control, it would be done well.

That still left who, when and where. The three questions would need to be answered quickly and simultaneously. The league left the decision of when to begin play to the two new franchises, though they would be requested

to come in at the same time. Initially, Huizenga had a "why wait" attitude, but he also wanted to make sure his organization was prepared when the first puck was dropped.

That meant he also had to get the "where" and the "who" solved fairly quickly. The NHL would allow South Florida and Southern California (as the franchises were called) to play in 1993-94 if they could prove they would be ready (read: they had a place to play and adequate time to form the team and front office).

The Miami Arena seemed to be the most logical place to play, at least to start, but the Miami Heat controlled the prime dates and all the amenities of the arena, and Huizenga made it clear he intended to build a new arena as soon as possible.

The day after the franchise was awarded, some of the calls received at the Blockbuster offices were regarding land and/or building expertise for a possible new arena. But with the 1993-94 season starting in less than 10 months, there would have to be an existing facility to house the team temporarily if there was any thought of playing in the 1993-94 season or the next one. An agreement on a lease needed to happen very quickly to give the league time to set up the expansion draft and the season schedule.

Spokesmen for the Miami Arena were excited about the possibility of having a hockey team paying rent checks. "We're delighted about getting hockey, obviously, and we think we can overcome any problems," Rob Franklin, vice president and CEO of the arena told the Fort Lauderdale *Sun-Sentinel* the day

 Bettman knew that Huizenga would run a first-class operation. It's the way he runs all his businesses, including his other pro-sports franchises—the Dolphins and the Marlins.

the franchise was awarded. Representatives of the Heat also expressed a desire to work with the hockey franchise to make the facility work for both teams.

"(The arena) seems to want hockey and that's the logical place to go," said Jim Blosser, former general manager of Huizenga Holdings. "Now it's a matter of sitting down to see if it works." Added Huizenga, "I'm hopeful we can work something out. I'm not talking financial terms, I'm talking about conditions; where we would put our team offices and the locker rooms, and the schedule."

One thing was certain. Even if Huizenga's team were to open in the Miami Arena, it would only be there for a short period of time. "The NHL doesn't feel hockey is economically feasible at the Miami Arena, and they prefer we build a state-of-the-art arena," Huizenga said at the time. It was a sentiment with which he wholeheartedly agreed.

Regarding the "who," early speculation included the much-traveled Mike Keenan as the first hire as general manager/coach. Ironically, on the day the story appeared on the front sports page of the Sun-Sentinel that Keenan was "excited" about the possibility of coming to South Florida, there was a box referring to a story inside that Roger Neilson was fired as coach of the New York Rangers.

"It would be exciting for a number of reasons," Keenan told Dave Joseph of the *Sun-Sentinel*. "First, the process of developing a team has been accelerated. Collective bargaining has made players more accessible to acquire.

Second, *I have the confidence in my ability to put together a team; to mold it and select the right people to work with me* (emphasis added). That's exciting to someone like me. And, third, Mr. Huizenga has proven in business and his other endeavors that he has the ability and resources to make things happen."

With Keenan having coached and left his second team since that statement, it is only speculation what would have happened had he been hired to run the Panthers, but Huizenga had his sights set elsewhere, both in terms of personnel and the entire process.

On January 5, 1993, the NHL Board of Governors met to discuss when and how the expansion draft would occur, where the two new franchises would select in the NHL entry draft. That was a critical point, and another good reason for the two new franchises to get ready for the 1993-94 season. The pool of draft-eligible amateurs was considered the deepest in years. Since there weren't going to be many potential superstars available in the expansion draft, no matter how the protection rules were formulated, the best place to get the future centerpiece of a franchise was the amateur draft.

The original proposal for the expansion draft was for each team to protect one goaltender, five defensemen and nine forwards. Players with one year of NHL experience or less were exempt. Those specifications were different from any of the previous drafts, including the drafts the previous two years when the San Jose Sharks (1991), Tampa Bay Lightning (1992) and Ottawa Senators (1992) built their franchises. In those drafts, each existing team protected two goaltenders and 14 skaters, with no positional preference. Also, players with two years or less of NHL experience were exempt.

A second phase of the proposed draft would help the other three new franchises. South Florida and Southern California could protect one goaltender, five defensemen and 10 forwards, and San Jose, Tampa and Ottawa would be allowed to select

from the remaining pool, though neither of the two newest teams could lose more than three players. The three other young teams would be assured of the first three picks in the amateur draft, if they finished with the three worst records. South Florida and Southern California would flip for the choice of drafting fourth or fifth.

While the marketing committee, headed by McNall, approved the policy, there was a group of owners who were decidedly against the proposal.

"If this goes through, you will have to ascertain your No. 1 goaltender for the next five to 10 years," said Bill Watters, the assistant general manager of the Toronto Maple Leafs. "You'll see a lot of activity around the trade deadline. The Rangers won't let (John) Vanbiesbrouck go to the Anaheim Ducks, and we're not going to let (Felix) Potvin go to the Miami Screaming Eagles, or whatever they're called."

Watters should get par-

tial credit for his predictions of trade activity regarding goaltenders, though apparently he didn't get his choice turned in in time for the "name the team" contest.

Despite the opposition, the plan was approved nine days later, and there was great incentive for the two franchises to begin playing as soon as possible.

After initially saying that he wanted the franchise to begin in the 1993-94 season, Huizenga wavered. He already had his hands full with the Marlins preparing for their inaugural season. "I feel a desire to get on the ice this year, but to do it right," he said. "We're not going to rush. I want this to be well thought out. We want to put the best product on the ice."

Looking back nearly four years later, he realizes that he was fortunate to pull it all off. "It was a little touchy for a while, because we were just getting ready to start baseball," he said. "We had a lot of work getting baseball ready, and all of a sudden, we have to get this hockey team together at the same time. Having just gone through the experience with the Marlins really helped us know how to handle the whole process. It was a lot of work, but our people did a really good job."

"I have the confidence in my ability to put together a team."

Finally, on January 26, Huizenga announced that if it were totally up to him, the team would start playing that fall. The only hurdle left to clear was signing a lease with the Miami Arena.

Early speculation on the team's first coach centered on many candidates, but Roger Neilson (left) was not among them. The Miami Arena (above) was not an ideal arena for hockey, especially since the Heat owned all the signage rights, but it would have to do.

"Hopefully we'll get it done in the next seven to 10 days," he said upon announcing his decision. But it took much longer. With the NHL's deadline of March 1 less than a week away, Huizenga and the Miami Sports and Exhibition Authority reached an agreement on lease terms on February 23. While Southern California did not have an agreement with the Anaheim Arena, South Florida had done all it could to begin play right away.

Of course, having made the decision to open play in less than eight months (early October), he had just more than four months before the expansion and amateur drafts, and he still didn't have an employee on the hockey side. Huizenga said that he had narrowed his choice of presidents to "two or three people, any of whom would be acceptable." He said the same thing regarding general managers, whose job it would be to hire a head coach.

Keenan had been eliminated as a choice for general manager, mostly because of his desire to coach the team as well. "If we're only going to have a short period of time to get this thing going, I want someone to be the general manager and someone to coach," he said. That decision left Philadelphia Flyers senior vice president Bob Clarke and Washington Capitals general manager David Poile as the two finalists for the job.

Clarke wanted it. Real bad. He was "rapping his knuckles on the desk" in Philadelphia, where he had had two previous tours. He was selected in the second round of the 1969 amateur draft by the Flyers. He spent 15 years with the team as a player, amassing 358 goals and 852 assists to be the team's all-time leading

> **"Having just gone through the experience with the Marlins really helped us know how to handle the whole process."**

scorer. He led the team to two straight Stanley Cup championships in the mid 70s, and when he retired, he was named the team's vice president and general manager.

In 1990, he was named to the same position with the Minnesota North Stars, who reached the Stanley Cup finals in his first season. But after his second year in Minneapolis, the lure of Philadelphia brought him back home. Unfortunately for him—fortunately for the Panthers—Clarke was a man with "a position and a title, but no job," according to an interview right before he was hired.

When Huizenga contacted Clarke, he knew he had to get back to a position with some punch.

"It was me looking for work that got me to see Mr. Huizenga, and I was fortunate that he was interested," he said. "I was working for the Flyers but not doing anything. The competitive fire was still burning. You miss being on the firing line when you've been there a long time.

"The thought of starting an expansion franchise was pretty exciting. I think if you want to manage, there always is an attraction of starting your own club. I guess anybody managing feels that he could start a club and do a good job."

Clarke got that chance on March 1, when Huizenga named Clarke the first employee in the team's history as the vice president and general manager of the team. "It was a very hard decision for me, because of our feelings for the Flyers," he said at the time. "I feel awful leaving, but I feel I want to manage again."

Huizenga knew he had hit the back of the net on this one. "He's just one heck of a guy," the owner said. "He's a real competitive person in everything he does."

Huizenga's team didn't have a name, uniforms, team colors or a logo, and Clarke didn't have an office, a secretary or even a telephone, but he hit the ground running. He was known as an aggressive player in his 15-year NHL Hall of Fame career, and he would have to be aggressive to accomplish all that lay ahead of him. He had to hire an entire staff, including scouts and coaches, draft and sign a team, and get them ready to play—all in seven months.

That decision was made final when the two new franchises officially accepted the invitation to open play in the 1993-94 season the day of the NHL's deadline. It was at that time that Eisner announced that his franchise would be called the Mighty Ducks after the popular Disney movie released in 1992.

While Huizenga's team still did not have a name, it did have a rival. Realignment of the NHL's divisions put South Florida in the Atlantic Division with the New York Rangers, New York Islanders, New Jersey Devils, Philadelphia Flyers, Washington Capitals and Tampa Bay Lightning. The Lightning had entered the league the previous season and had the vast market of Florida all to itself. Now it would have to share the state with Huizenga's squad.

The fact that it was Huizenga made the team easier to hate. Huizenga was viewed as a bad guy in the Tampa Bay market. There was rumor that Huizenga had been behind the movement to block the San Francisco Giants' (major league baseball) move to the area. Huizenga also informed the public that his team wouldn't be called "Miami" or "Fort Lauderdale" Anything. The designation would be "South Florida," or worse yet to the fans in Tampa, "Florida."

"Overall, this is positive for us," said Mel Lowell, the Lightning's executive vice president. "The people of Tampa already know Mr. Huizenga, and I'm sure the rivalry will be instant."

Phil Esposito, a fellow NHL Hall of Famer whose career overlapped Clarke's, scooped up the rivalry puck and fired it right at Clarke's new employers. "Now we've got somebody our fans can really hate," he said.

That would be easier once the South Florida franchise was named. Huizenga ran a name-the-team contest and more than 6,000 people responded. There were familiar enough sounding names like the "Miami Ice." But that was ruled out because Huizenga didn't want to use a city name. Some people tried the humorous approach, but the "South Florida Barricades," with orange and white striped uniforms in honor of the common roadside apparatus and its garb, also were ruled out.

The overwhelming choice for a name was "Florida Panthers." The Florida panther was named the state animal of Florida in 1982. It is one of 13 subspecies of the cougar/mountain lion and has some distinct characteristics that its cousins in the west and other regions don't have.

In the late 1800s, there was a bounty on panther heads. That thinned their population considerably. Then, with the human population growth taking away from the cats' roaming space—each cat needs an extreme amount of its own space—there was a lot of cross

Bob Clarke (left) was "rapping his knuckles on the desk" in boredom in Philadelphia in his role as the Flyers' senior vice president, so he jumped at the opportunity to work for Wayne Huizenga as the vice president and general manager of the as-yet unnamed team.

breeding among the different subspecies that nearly extinguished the *Felis Concolor Coryi*— the Florida panther. It was among the first animals included in the first Endangered Species Act enacted by the federal government in 1973. Yet when the name was chosen, it was estimated that there were only between 30 and 50 Florida panthers in the wild.

Once the name was selected and unveiled to the public, Huizenga instituted several programs that would help replenish the panther population. Through his Blockbuster stores and the National Fish and Wildlife Foundation, more than $50,000 was raised immediately for panther aid. Blockbuster also produced a hockey-education video, with the proceeds going to the fund.

> **Huizenga instituted several programs that would help replenish the panther population.**

"We felt that if we were going to take its name, we might as well bring some awareness to it," said Greg Bouris, the team's first director of public relations. "Not that it would be the life-long calling of the franchise to be out there trying to help these cats, but we felt that it should be a priority for our first year in existence to do what we could." The team also instituted the "Panther Saves Help Save the Panther" program, where individuals could donate money for every save by Panthers goalies during the season.

Of course, that would only help if Panthers goaltenders were good. True to his word, Clarke's first two employees were scouts—Dennis Patterson as Chief Scout and Ron Harris as Eastern Scout. Shortly thereafter, Huizenga announced Bill Torrey as the team's president.

Torrey was involved in the building of two expansion franchises, the second with remarkable success. He was an aggressive administrator who had a plan and stuck by it.

"In looking for a president, I must have talked to 100 people, and somewhere along the way in the conversation, Bill Torrey's name always came up," Huizenga said. "Then Nelson Doubleday (owner of the New York Mets) called me and said, 'Have you ever heard of Bill Torrey?' I said, 'Yes, his name comes up all the time.' He said, 'You wouldn't go wrong by hiring Bill Torrey.'

"When I interviewed him, I liked his personality and I liked his age. He is mature. I liked his track record, someone who could come down here and deal with this media. You always hear about the New York media being the worst sports media in the country. Well, all those guys have moved down here now. So this is a real tough media market, and we needed somebody who had some age to him, and somebody who could come in here and have credibility to make this thing work. Torrey fit the bill."

Torrey began his NHL career in 1969 as the executive vice president of the expansion California Seals. The Seals were part of the six-team expansion in 1967. After three years in California, Torrey joined the New York Islanders as that team's first general manager in 1972.

The Islanders didn't do very well in their first year, amassing just 30 points with a 12-60-6 record. But within three seasons, the Islanders were in the playoffs, becoming the second team in professional sports history to come back from a 3-0 deficit in a seven-game series to claim the series. After pulling off the feat against Pittsburgh in 1975, the Isles almost did it again in their next series, losing to

Philadelphia in the seventh game after winning three straight to erase a 3-0 deficit.

In 1980, the Islanders stopped Montreal's four-year run as Stanley Cup champions with Bob Nystrom's overtime goal against Philadelphia. That started a four-year run of their own for the Islanders. Torrey built the Islanders with defense, speed, character and, most importantly, good goaltending. It was the blueprint he planned to use to build the Panthers.

"The first thing that you have to do is have a program," Torrey said. "There are no two eras that are exactly the same. The Islanders began in '72 and now we're many years hence. But there are certain things that you try to do and stick by. If your planning and your thinking is right initially, it will work. You have to have the courage of your own convictions, and you have to have the good plan going in. Obviously the key to that is making the best assessments that you can on what's available.

"In starting the Islanders, obviously the expansion draft was not near what we got in the Panthers draft, in terms of overall quality. On the other hand, the early years of the amateur draft were far better than what we're getting now. You have to work around those facts.

"In '72, you could tell after the first four or five players you basically were getting minor league players. We got an Eddie Westfall and players of that quality in the first few rounds, whereas in our draft here, we felt that there would be players of major league skill almost all the way through. In other words, we felt we would have a nucleus of a team. Obviously there were no 50- or 60-goal scorers out there, but there were a lot of players who had major league experience and good major league skills—the most obvious being in goaltending.

There were quality goal keepers available for us, which was not true in '72."

With Torrey and Clarke on board, the on-ice foundation was laid. But Huizenga knew he needed somebody to run the organization off the ice. He also knew he had the right guy for the job already on board. Dean Jordan was the vice president of communications for the Marlins and had just completed the expansion process with the new baseball franchise. Two days after Torrey was hired, Jordan moved over to the Panthers to assume the role of vice pres-

There were many roles to fill as the calendar steamed toward opening night. Jordan (left) was moved from the Marlins to run the business side of the franchise. Torrey (right) ran the hockey side,. That left Stanley C. Panther in charge of charging up the new fans.

Wayne Huizenga

Wayne Huizenga is on record as saying he thought hockey could work in South Florida. While most so-called "experts" thought the winter sport had as much chance of succeeding in the balmy climes of the Miami metro area as the proverbial snowball in hades, the Panthers' owner thought differently.

Huizenga knew his territory. He had lived in South Florida for 43 years, and he knew that most residents of the area were not natives. Many were from the northern east coast of the United States where the National Hockey League had been successful for years. Others came south from Canada, where the sport was perfected. With that information in his pocket, Huizenga was willing to risk his own money to test his theory, and he was awarded an NHL franchise.

Four years removed from that decision, Huizenga's hunch looks dead-solid perfect. The Panthers are successful on the ice—reaching the Stanley Cup finals in their third season and the playoffs in two of their first four—and off the ice, where the team's jersey still ranks as one of the best sellers in the league merchandising race.

The success starts at the top, because Huizenga is willing to let the credit flow down. "Right from the start I liked Mr. Huizenga a lot," said Bob Clarke, the team's first general manager. "He was always very honest and very up front. You could tell he had the intention of having a good hockey club.

"Everything we needed was provided. We had to pay players a lot of money, and that was fine with him. We were allowed to get the players we needed to be a good club."

Huizenga hired good people, who then hired other good people, and then Huizenga let them do their jobs. "For me it's very easy to stay out of it," Huizenga said. "I'm so busy doing other things; I'm running 18 hours a day as it is. I'm very pleased that I have people like (president Bill) Torrey and (general manager) Bryan (Murray) to run the show. I can go to the games as a fan. I don't have to go three hours before the game.

"I run the other teams (he also owns MLB's Florida Marlins and the NFL's Miami Dolphins) exactly the same."

Huizenga's personal story is much like his hockey team's. He worked hard, caught a few breaks along the way, and then worked hard again.

He was born and raised near Chicago, and moved to South Florida when he was a freshman in high school. After high school, he spent a year and a half at Calvin College in Grand Rapids, Michigan. He decided the cold Michigan winters were too much and returned home. "I thought I'd just sit out the rest of the school year and then go to the University of Miami. Some friends of mine decided to join the Army Reserves, so I did that, too. When I got out of the Army Reserves, I came home and was going to go back to school, but the first day I was home, I happened to bump into a friend of my father in a restaurant.

"He owned a small, three-truck refuse company in Pompano Beach and he had to fire his manager. He asked me to be an emergency replacement. So I went to work for him for 'a week or two' until he could get someone else. Two years later I was still there, and I finally left and bought my own truck and went in business for myself."

That was in 1962. By 1971, the business covered the state of Florida. His cousin, who was managing a waste-management company in Chicago, offered to merge the companies and six months later the company went public. Today, WNX Technologies covers 41 countries around the world and generates $10 to $12 billion per year.

With that kind of track record, when Huizenga speaks, people are bound to listen. Yet those people who work for him say he doesn't insist on his way. "He is the ultimate sports owner," Murray says. "He allows you to do your thing and he doesn't second-guess you. He offers help if you need help, but he allows Bill and me to run the franchise.

"The treatment he has displayed to the players, the interest he has in the team, the enthusiasm that he and his wife have, the outings and social functions we've had because of this kind of owner, really have brought this team a long way as far as respecting what goes on in the franchise.

"When you see him beaming because we've won a game, or you see him on television commenting on the group of guys we have, there is no questions that he's a tremendous bonus to the players. That just doesn't happen in other cities."

John Vanbiesbrouck, the team's first pick in the expansion draft that began the team, says the players feel good about their owner. "He's been great for us," the Beezer said. "It might be the only time in sports that the players have convinced the owner to like a sport (he didn't know anything about). He has convinced South Florida to like hockey. That is big to the players because we could have been shuffled off somewhere with all the stuff that was going on. But he was willing to lose $15 or $30 million a year. That's pretty convincing."

That will change when the new arena is finished in Sunrise. The team will receive the lion's share of the revenues from the facility, instead of having to watch the NBA's Miami Heat cash the checks.

But Huizenga doesn't concern himself just with making money. Yes, it's important. It's how he's able to do so much for his community and region. But love for the community supersedes the financial losses. He's willing to play his hunches. He's willing to use his resources to promote South Florida.

He's also not too concerned about getting any credit. "Shortly after we got the Marlins—we hadn't even played our first game yet—I went to the Honda Classic golf tournament here, and some guy came up to me and asked for my autograph," he said. "Autograph? What would he want with my autograph? It never dawned on me that I would sign an autograph. That's for the players. Everywhere I went, I started signing autographs. That was a strange feeling."

Not any stranger than hockey being a booming success in South Florida.

● *Huizenga achieved much of his success in business by hiring qualified people and letting them do what they were hired to do. He promised to do the same with South Florida's hockey team.*

ident of business and marketing. In that role he was responsible for the day-to-day business operations of the club.

"The only ice people see down here is in their drinks."

"Having just gone through the expansion process with the Marlins helped Dean know how to handle it," Huizenga said. "He still remained an officer with the Marlins, because of his expertise in broadcasts. Bill was able to leave most of the business-side stuff to Dean, so he could focus more on the team building with

Bob Clarke. That allowed Bill to spend the necessary time evaluating talent with Bob, which was a big reason we drafted so well."

With most of the staff on board, there still was a monumental task. The success of a franchise often can be traced to the support of the local crowd. South Florida hardly could be considered a "hotbed"—or would that be "icebed"?—of hockey. The public relations and merchandising staffs had to win the attention of the 4 million-plus people in the tri-county area and teach them the game of hockey.

Many of the residents of the area had moved from the northeastern United States, and there were a lot of people from Canada, but it was critical that Bouris and Ron Dennis, the director of merchandising, would be able to convert those general hockey fans into Florida Panthers fans. But each time a big event occurred for the franchise, it seemed that another sports event overshadowed it.

The Florida Marlins began their first season in the National League on April 5, 1993, to a packed house at Joe Robbie Stadium. Charlie Hough picked up the win, Brian Harvey notched the save and the Marlins beat the Los Angeles Dodgers, 6-3, in front of 42,334 of their closest friends. While the Panthers were trying to make a splash in the market, baseball was being played in Florida during the regular season for the first time after years of spring training action.

"The hype surrounding the Marlins' beginning was phenomenal," said Bouris, who arrived in Miami shortly after the Marlins played their first game. "I wondered if we were even going to make a ripple. How was hockey going to work out here. People kept saying, 'The only ice people see down here is in their drinks.'"

The Marlins stole the Panthers' thunder again in June when on the day of the expansion draft to stock the hockey team, the Marlins traded for slugger Gary Sheffield. Even the Panthers first-ever regular-season game was somewhat overshadowed. The game, in Chicago, came on the evening of Michael Jordan's retirement from basketball.

"We went to Chicago to get ready to play the game. We went to the hotel and turned on the TV and there were all the bulletins that the Chicago Bulls were holding a press conference the following day—the day of our game—that Michael Jordan was going to announce his retirement. You have to be kidding.

"We went to our morning skate, and only one of the television crews that came up from Florida was there. The media has been great to us. They've traveled with us and covered all our big happenings. But this was a coup for them. I'm sure, outside of Chicago, the best coverage on Michael Jordan's retirement came from the South Florida media. Talk about being overshadowed. The whole day was overshadowed. We walked into Chicago Stadium for our morning skate, and we could have been anywhere. We could have been in Egypt."

Back home in Egypt, uh, South Florida, the Panthers were hotter than the Sahara. To a large extent, that was due to some intensive efforts by the staff. "When we finally were fully staffed, we had exactly 100 days before the season opener, and we had to build a franchise," Bouris said. "As the media relations director, I had to find out who was in sports coverage for radio, television, whatever. We also had to produce publications and build relationships within the community.

"It was a group effort. It wasn't 'Media, go do your thing. Promotions, go do your thing. Corporate sales, go do your thing. Merchandising, go do your thing.' We had meetings every Monday morning at 8 a.m. We would say, 'Here's what we're going to do. How does media fit into the equation.' We would do that with each department. Together we could build up awareness, through corporate advertising, sponsorships, T-shirts and other merchandise, our guides, and a caravan with six or seven players.

"One thing we were very careful about was avoiding the term 'expansion.' We didn't want to use the term because with expansion comes kind of a safety net for failure. 'We don't have to be good, we're an expansion team.' So we used the words 'first-year.'

"It was a great situation to work in. Wayne Huizenga, with his vision, his before-you-say-no-say-why-not attitude, pervades all through his entities. It allows you to be a risk taker. You may do some things and they may backfire. They may not work, but you've learned why they don't work. You also learn that if you take a risk, it comes with a greater potential reward.

And that is the best environment in which to do business."

Risk taking on the ice could result in a goal for the opponent. Risk taking in deciding whether to change the cover of the game program for every home game—as Bouris was able to do—could result in losing a little money. But both types of risk reflect the larger picture. Huizenga was willing to hire qualified people to run the hockey side of his franchise, and

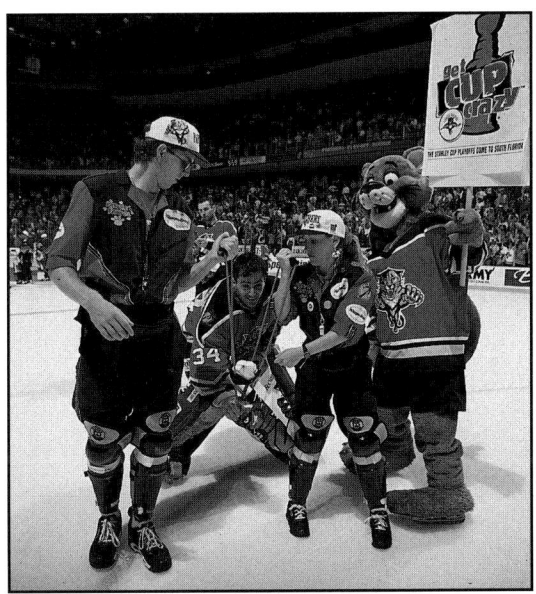

then let them do it. He ran the business side of his franchise in an equally positive manner. Greg Cote of the Miami Herald wrote, "Wayne will own it the right way, first-class, champagne, and therefore we love him. Anything he does is A-OK with us."

Pretty strong talk from the usually cynical media. But Huizenga exudes and inspires confidence. It may be his Midas Touch. Consider the way he made his fortune. You know, "One

Bouris (left) credits Huizenga with creating a "great situation to work in" because he allows his people to take risks. In media relations, that may mean changing the cover of the game-day program, or it may mean introducing special features like the Panther Patrol (above).

Man's Garbage Is Another Man's Treasure"? Huizenga took a one-truck garbage route and built it into the world's largest sanitation company. In 1987, he bought the rights to Blockbuster Entertainment when there were just 19 Blockbuster Video stores dotting the countryside. In six years, the company had grown to more than 3,500 stores.

Entertainment was a key word with the Panthers. "I think the entertainment started when we were competitive right off the bat,"

Bouris said. "Every game was close." But it was more than the team. The marketing department unveiled a mascot, Stanley C. Panther, to appeal to the kids. The "Panther Patrol" would be used to entertain the crowd during intermissions, sliding across the ice and sling-shotting T-shirts into the crowd. A Panther growl would accompany the cheers following Florida goals.

Things were beginning to get rolling.

"Very few of those things were unique," Bouris said, "but they have to be done right."

Making the right choice of colors was a big decision for the Panthers. The logo had been designed and every conceivable color combination had been considered. "We tried every color that somebody had whispered to Wayne as the next pop color," Bouris said. "We looked at pea green, lime green, everything imaginable. We tried sublimation logos where the whole sweater was one big logo." It came down to the "in" color combination—teal, silver, purple and black—and a more traditional combination of red, navy blue and gold.

Huizenga was in favor of the teal combination. Jordan and Clarke also favored that choice. Torrey and Bouris were all for the red, blue and gold. Obviously, Huizenga had the final choice, but he was willing to listen to other people's thoughts. He brought Blockbuster employees into the conference room and showed them the two combinations. The vote was 50/50.

"A lot of the people who liked the teal were from South Florida," Bouris said. "That is a very South Floridian color. The Marlins use a version of it. The Dolphins use a version of it. But I found it a little on the trendy side. Everybody who had come along recently had used it. When I looked at the red, navy and gold, I thought, 'Everything old becomes new again. Now these colors look fresh in light of the trendy ones.'"

The day came for the decision to be made. Torrey and Jordan were in New York, and they were prepared to visit the designers to give them the final decision. Bouris was a little depressed, because he figured the teal combination was going to win. But just before the call came from New York, Huizenga had a change of heart. Bouris recalled the situation. "He looked down and said, 'That red looks pretty sharp. I have to admit that it looks really fresh, and the cat really jumps up at you more.' Bob Clarke said, 'You know, the more I look at it, the more I think the players would really like to wear that color scheme.'

"I was saying to myself, 'Don't say a word. Just nod.' Then Wayne decided, 'Let's go with the red.' He felt bad because Bill and Dean weren't involved with the decision. We decid-

Whoever convinced whom, the red, blue and gold became the team's colors.

"You don't know how well received the other one would have been," Bouris said. "But even to this day our logo is among the sales leaders. You knew it would do well during our

ed that when they called we would string them along. When they called, Bill was pleading for the red. Wayne said, 'Okay, it's the red.' I'm sure Bill wanted to hurry and get off the phone before Wayne changed his mind."

Torrey recalls the other end of the conversation. "We were in Commissioner (Gary) Bettman's office," he said. "We called Wayne. When Bettman said 'Red,' we said 'Red,' and Wayne said, 'Okay, the red looks great.'"

expansion year, because we were new. But everybody still comments that our road sweaters are among the best, if not the best, in the game."

Things were beginning to get rolling. The marketing plan was in place. People in South Florida were being

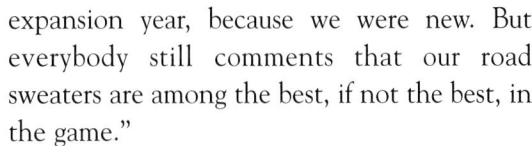

It's a team effort, as (left photo, from left) Torrey, Clarke, Jordan and Huizenga take a "slice of the ice." The red, navy blue and gold combination (above) won out over the teal, silver, purple and black. The Panthers' sweater remains one of the best sellers in the NHL.

approached and taught to love hockey. The team had a name and uniforms. The next step was to name a coach. On April 27, the story broke that Clarke had discussed the position with Neilson, the former Rangers coach.

"They took ... guys who were good workers and made them into a real good team."

"I'm interested in being back as a coach of a National Hockey League team," he told David Neal of *The Miami Herald*. "I think it would be exciting and a different kind of challenge than taking over an established team."

"It certainly was a case of me needing a job," he said recently when looking back on the situation, "but I liked the idea of working with an expansion team. I heard that Bobby Clarke was a top guy to work with."

Neilson was a popular choice in hockey circles. He was an aggressive coach, who specialized in defense. He had spent most of the previous 27 years in coaching. He had coached the Rangers to their best finish in 50 years in 1991-92, when they earned 105 points and won their first division title since 1942. Neilson was seen as a players coach. But a slow start in 1992 led to his firing. He didn't see eye-to-eye with Rangers star Mark Messier, and it cost him.

Yet he seemed to be a perfect fit for an expansion team. He was big on team chemistry and a physical style that would be suited to a team that was not likely to have a prolific scorer. The Panthers certainly thought he would fit their plan.

In fact, Clarke believes the success the Panthers enjoyed in year No. 3 mostly was the result of the work put in by Neilson and his assistants. "In my opinion, the reason the Panthers became a good club so quickly was Roger, Craig Ramsey, Tom Webster and Lindy

Ruff," he said. "They took the Brian Skrudlands and the Scott Mellanbys and Gord Murphys, guys who were good workers and made them into a real good team.

"Guys like Bill Lindsay couldn't get playing time (with Quebec), and now everybody would love to have Bill Lindsay. Tom Fitzgerald had been up and down and kicked around by the Islanders and they didn't even want him. Now everybody would love to have Tom. We took those guys because they were available to us, and we knew they had a good work ethic, but the credit should be given to the coaches."

Neilson won't take all the credit. He passes it along to players.

"We wanted character players and we wanted speed. We got both," he said. "I don't know that you could ever duplicate that draft again. I'm sure there was some luck involved. We got almost all the players we wanted. They all

turned out to be as good or better than we had thought. Right from the start it was a gritty team. It certainly was a great coaching experience, because it was a coach's dream to have players like that."

Oh yeah, players. The day Neilson was hired, June 2, was three weeks and a day before the expansion draft, the Panthers' first opportunity to stock their roster. The lenient protection rules approved in mid-January allowed the Panthers and the Mighty Ducks to build a solid foundation immediately, but that would occur only if the right players were chosen. That meant a lot of work to draft the team that Torrey and Clarke could manage and Neilson could coach.

"One advantage that we had was that Bob Clarke and I had a very similar philosophy," Torrey said. "We never disagreed about anything relative to preparing for the draft. We ran a number of mock drafts. We went through it time and time again to see what we would end up with. We not only did a mock draft of who we wanted, but we also analyzed very carefully what we thought Anaheim would do. We looked at players that (Ducks general manager) Jack Ferreira had drafted in the past. We spent a lot of time going over what we thought they would do, because no matter what you may want to do, if you're not prepared for what the other guy is going to do, you're not going to end up getting the players you want anyway."

The mock drafts teamed up three people to a side, switching teams to get every possible combination. The mock drafts, and the research to prepare for them revealed a deep talent pool. "We saw very quickly that there were a number of players who had some real skills," Torrey said. "Though there were no high-scoring offensive players, there were players who came and worked hard every night, players who would not buckle under, players who would never take a backward step."

There are a lot of words that describe that type of player. "Character" comes up often. "Tough" is commonly used. But there is one word that seems to

be used the most with the Florida Panthers, especially the original players.

Grit.

"To me it describes determination," Clarke said. "It describes the guy who can get knocked on his (rear) and get up and keep coming back. That's what (Dave) Lowry is, that's what (Brian) Skrudland is, that's what Gord Murphy is, that's what (Scott) Mellanby is.

"I don't consider fighting toughness. It's part of the game, and you have to have guys who can do that. But for me, toughness is the guy who, when the puck is in the corner, will go get it regardless of whether he's going to get splattered. It's going in front of the net where you know someone is going to cross-check you. That's the type of player we were after, and the type we thought we had."

Each had come from a situation where he was not protected by his original club, for a number of reasons. Some, like Skrudland, were

Huizenga and Neilson (left) celebrate their selections in the expansion draft that brought them 10 players who played key roles in the run to the Stanley Cup Finals three years later. (Above) Neilson explains the team's strategy to the press after the draft concludes.

coming off injuries that potentially could have limited their effectiveness. Others, like Mellanby, were unprotected because their teams thought their salaries exceeded their contribution. Still others, like Lindsay, were stuck behind depth and their teams felt it would take too long for them to contribute.

"I don't think there is any doubt that it had an effect," said Mike Hough, who played with the Quebec Nordiques for seven years before expansion brought him to Florida. "We all wanted to prove that we still were NHL players and that our teams had made a mistake."

John Vanbiesbrouck took a different approach. "I don't think we wanted to prove to the teams that let us go as much as we wanted to prove to each other that we could play at a top level," he said. "We wanted to gain respect. It's no different from any other team at the start of the season. Just because a team has a Lemieux, a Gretzky, a Messier, doesn't mean it is going to get instantaneous respect in a team-oriented game."

Either way, the talent assembled in the draft meant the Panthers were going to be tough to beat. "We didn't have those players a week and we had teams calling," Clarke said. "We had one team calling us where we were doing the draft, trying to trade for one of our players."

The key was goaltending. Heading into the day of the draft, most of the speculation was that the Panthers would select Vanbiesbrouck if they won the coin flip for the first pick. He was a member of the Vancouver Canucks by way of a last-minute trade with the

> ## "We all wanted to prove that we still were NHL players and that our teams had made a mistake."

Rangers. Neilson had coached Vanbiesbrouck with the Rangers, and he did not hide his preference. "He was certainly my first pick all along," he said. "If I remember correctly, there was some question the day before that maybe we would go for somebody else. I remember I was shocked when I heard about that. I said, 'Surely we are not considering that,' and they didn't. But I think he was the fairly obvious number one.

"He was our mealticket. He was our only superstar, and the challenge was there for him, and he really responded to it. He kept us in there. We were really lucky to have Mark Fitzpatrick (from the Islanders with the second pick), too, because Bill Torrey knew him well. While I don't believe Mark has been really happy to have been a backup all this time, he's been a great backup. He can go in and come up with huge games, so the combination of Beezer and Mark was just terrific. You couldn't ask for anything more. They won us game after game."

The Panthers also drafted a goaltender with their third pick—Daren Puppa of the Maple Leafs—who was picked up the next day by the Lightning in Phase II of the draft. The team then followed those picks with eight straight defensemen—according the structure of the draft—including Paul Laus of the Penguins and Murphy from Dallas, two players who still toil for the Panthers. Torrey believes the old adage that "defense wins championships." "No matter how good your goaltending is, if you're giving up 40 to 50 shots a night, you're not going to win," he said. "The one area where people don't give our team enough credit is with our defense. Then we have Vanbiesbrouck and Fitzpatrick on top of that."

It was not until Tom Fitzgerald was taken with the team's 12th pick (24th overall) that a front-line player was chosen. Jesse Belanger and Scott Levins were next, followed by five players who remained with the team through the first four years: Mellanby, Skrudland, Hough, Lowry and Lindsay.

In all, 10 players who were selected on that day were with the team as it opened its fourth season. Add Rob Niedermayer, the team's first entry-draft selection, Jody Hull, who was signed as a free agent a month and a half later,

and Stu Barnes, who was picked up a month into the first season, and there were 13 players—more than half the active roster. To keep that many players on the same team for four seasons is pretty remarkable in today's age of free agency. To have that many from the first team, well, that is amazing.

"I think that says something about the people who scouted us off the bat and about the

commitment that the guys who were picked up have made to each other and made to the organization," Skrudland said. "As a result I think the organization has been fair back to us as well, not to just bring in youth, but to win with what we have. We've been very successful from day one. We've been stepping it up and getting a little bit better with each acquisition.

"Also, I think each and every individual has come to play for himself, play for some self pride, play for individuality, which is going to make you better. Because if you are a better player, then your team is going to be better. We've got a phrase around: "big team, little me." You've got to come play every game, every shift. We've all been very committed that way."

The Panthers were thrilled with their haul. "In comparing the two drafts, naturally you like the guys you pick, that's why you pick them," Neilson said. "But I thought our team was far superior to Anaheim when the draft was over. I just felt we got the best of what was available."

While the expansion draft established the present, the NHL entry draft set the future in motion. The National Hockey League's Central Scouting Bureau, which rates only North American players, had five players listed as "top players." "It's a deep draft," CSB director Frank Bonello said. "It's not limited to the first five players. Usually you have the top few who are top players. But when you consider the European players, you're going to the top eight or 10 this year. It's a deep year."

Through some wheeling and dealing, the Panthers got a "top player" and some depth. Niedermayer, described as a "ready-to-play

Torrey (above) waved good-bye to the easy chair he had earned as the architect of the New York Islanders dynasty in the early '80s. Instead, he chose to try again with the Panthers.

NHL forward," was taken with the team's first pick, the fifth overall. The Panthers won another coin flip with Anaheim and chose to pass on the fourth pick, and thereby earned the top pick overall in the 1994 draft.

But by taking Niedermayer, the player Clarke and Neilson wanted to begin with, the Panthers were able to secure an extra pick. It shook down like this. Ottawa took Alexandre Daigle with the first pick. San Jose traded the second pick to Hartford (sixth overall), who chose Chris Pronger. San Jose wanted Russian forward Viktor Kozlov, and the only team that stood in its way was the Panthers. Although Florida was not real interested in Kozlov, Clarke told Hartford general manager Brian Burke that the Panthers might trade that pick to somebody who was.

"Part of San Jose's deal was that the Russian had to be there," Clarke said at the time. "We used that knowledge." Hartford wanted to make sure that San Jose got Kozlov, so the trade wouldn't cost the Whalers its first- and second-round picks in 1994 in addition to the sixth pick in 1993 that they already surrendered. Just to be safe, Burke traded his second-round pick in the 1994 draft to the Panthers for the assurance that the Panthers wouldn't trade the pick or select Kozlov.

Tampa Bay selected Chris Gratton third overall, and Anaheim chose Paul Kariya with the fourth-overall pick. That left the Panthers up with the fifth pick overall. "In this draft, we thought only two players (Niedermayer and Pronger) could step in right away," Torrey said at the draft. "(Rob) is probably as close to

> ## "There was a large segment of the population who had left hockey behind in New York, Chicago, Boston, Detroit, Philadelphia.

being ready to play in the NHL as anyone in the draft. He's physically strong, and he's an extraordinary skater, the best skater in the draft."

Niedermayer, the younger brother of New Jersey Devils defenseman Scott, the third pick in the 1991 draft, was pleased to be selected. "It's a big jump, trying to play in the NHL, but this is a good opportunity to start my career," he said. "I'm going to try my best to step in and play this year."

The Panthers, obviously, were not through drafting, and Clarke was not through dealing. Clarke dealt the Panthers' second-round pick (31st overall) to Winnipeg for the Jets' second-round (41st) and third-round (67th) selections. Combine those picks with the extra third-round pick they had from Tampa for agreeing to select Puppa in the expansion draft (so the Lightning could take him the next day in Phase II), and the Panthers ended up with five picks in the first three rounds.

With their second-round pick, the Panthers selected goaltender Kevin Weeks. The three third-round picks netted them defensemen Chris Armstrong and Mikael Tjallden and center Steve Washburn. Weeks, Armstrong and Washburn still are in the system, and Tjallden's rights are owned by the team, though he currently is playing in Sweden.

The players were the final piece of the puzzle, though Torrey said the team he left Quebec City with was not likely to be the same one with which he started training camp. The final 100 days had started, and all the new players had to be introduced to the fans of South Florida. Many of those fans had moved from the north, where they were exposed to hockey previously. Many others were starting from scratch. "There was a large segment of the population who had left hockey behind in New York, Chicago, Boston, Detroit, Philadelphia.

We knew we would need those people to help sustain us during the first year," Bouris said. "Whenever teams from those markets came in, you would see old Gordie Howe sweaters, old Bruins sweaters, old Flyers sweaters.

"We also knew that if we were going to be successful, we had to create new fans. We had to create an environment that was going to be exciting."

To get the word out about this new team, the Panthers organized a "fan caravan" around the Miami-Fort Lauderdale-Palm Beach area. Seven players, including Vanbiesbrouck, Niedermayer, Lowry, Mellanby and Skrudland, toured the area introducing fans to hockey, and more importantly, to themselves.

The fans found out that these players were real. They were personable. They were approachable. "We started with something that may have been inquisitive and transformed it into a sense of partnership," Bouris said. "The fans felt, 'It's our team and we're a part of it.'

"People felt that they could go out and touch the product. After games, when the players would leave the arena, they would sign autographs. Every practice is open to the public. After practice, people would wait for the players, who would come out and say hello. They guys were very good about it. We became 'The Franchise You Can Touch.'"

While the logistics of the practice facility and the Miami Arena allowed the fans access to the players, the type of player helped, too. "There have been a lot of reporters I've known over the years from all

the different teams I've been with who would come up to me and say, 'Those are the best guys,'" said Neilson, who now, in St. Louis, is with his seventh NHL team.

"I think we were fortunate that without really knowing too many of the players personally, we ended up having good people and good families, players who were all low-maintenance type of players," Clarke added.

"They were willing to work to sell the sport in the community, and they were not

looking for anything out of it personally. I think that players like Vanbiesbrouck, Mellanby, Skrudland, all of them, would go out and do what was necessary and do it properly and do it with decency and humility. I think that's fairly rare in professional sports now. Players, if they go out, want to be paid and they want to be treated like superstars. These guys didn't. These guys were outstanding."

There was some question how the population of South Florida would embrace hockey, but from the beginning, the Panthers had no problem filling the arena with enthusiastic fans.

These guys quickly were becoming outstanding on the ice as well. The Panthers hired Billy Smith, the Hall of Famer goaltender who spent 18 years in the NHL, most of them with the New York Islanders. Smith backstopped the Islanders' four straight Stanley Cup championships. He coaches the Panthers goalies, Vanbiesbrouck and Fitzpatrick, as well as the top prospects in the system.

Without really knowing too many of the players personally, we ended up having good people and good families.

"Billy can't help you win or lose. That's just too far of a reach for a coach to come and have that much of an influence," Vanbiesbrouck said. "But he gives you little insights on what he thinks might help you. Then you take it and go with it. The best attribute of Billy is that he lets you go with one thought rather than a million. 'You're doing this, you're doing that.' Instead, he'll say, 'Let's just concentrate on one thing.' If it works out, he will be the first one to tell you, 'Good game,' or 'Bad game,' or 'I think you should have done this.'

"It's fun to bump something off of a guy like him. Billy is a unique person. He got it done four times. I don't think that anybody, at least in my pads, will ever question Billy Smith. And inspiration from a guy like that doesn't hurt either."

While the expansion draft and the amateur draft stocked the team with most of its players, both for the present and the future, there still were some holes to fill. True to his word, Torrey signed 12 free agents and made the club's first trade before training camp opened. One of those free agents, Jody Hull, still was a valuable contributor to the team during the team's fourth season.

"Jody has become one of the premier checking wingers in the league," Neilson said. "On top of that, he scored 20 goals (in 1995-96). He's a guy whose career has really taken an upturn."

Torrey added another man who had turned in an outstanding career—a Hall of Fame career. It's too bad his playing career was done by the time the Panthers got ahold of him, but Denis Potvin, the cornerstone of Torrey's Islanders dynasty was hired in August as the analyst on the television broadcasts. Potvin, a defenseman, was the first pick overall in 1973, the Islanders' second season. The similarities between the two franchises is striking, according to Potvin.

"We reached the semifinals in our third season, just like the Panthers did," he said. "The difference was that they won Game 7 in Pittsburgh, where we lost. That sets them apart. But the team was very much the same. There weren't a lot of superstars on our 1975 team. Bryan Trottier wasn't there. Mike Bossy wasn't there. John Tonelli wasn't there.

"Of course, the architect of that team is the same guy who is the architect here. Just look at the draft choices. Billy Harris was a forward who was the first player taken, like Rob Niedermayer. The first pick in the second year was a defenseman (Ed Jovanovski), just like I was.

"The one key word in both franchises was 'character.' This is the No. 1 attribute that Bill Torrey has always looked for. That certainly is how the Islanders were built and it looks very much the same here."

Training camp for this team finally came on September 10. In a way, it must have seemed like forever. At the same time, it must have seemed like a split-second. "Everything we did from a marketing standpoint, a media relations standpoint, a sales standpoint, was done by the book," Bouris said. "We used very solid, sound practices, sports business practices, great models. Established and new teams call us for ideas and recommendations. The staff went through a lot to put together the franchise in 100 days.

"But I think that may have helped, because

going to the net hard. When you watched the 60 guys who were at camp all doing exactly the same thing, you knew that it was going to be something special. We seemed to jell really quickly."

That jelling goes back to the quality of the players. "When you have goalies like John

we didn't have a year to get soft. We had 100 days. I know we had the blinders on. We did only what we had to do, and that allowed us to focus. Our focus was pretty sharp and narrow."

Once that training camp opened, it was very obvious very quickly that this team was going to be better than the outside "experts" thought. "We saw that they really had done their homework right from the beginning," Gord Murphy said. "They had drafted players that were known for being tough. Not necessarily that they were fighters, but they came in and competed every night and worked hard. When we saw that, we were pretty excited."

Hull said it began with the first intra-squad scrimmage. "Guys were banging, fighting,

Vanbiesbrouck and Mark Fitzpatrick available, all of a sudden you've got two quality goaltenders in the net," Dave Lowry said. "Then you have the leaders who were available, the Brian Skrudlands, the Scott Mellanbys, the Mike Houghs, the Tom Fitzgeralds. The list just keeps going on and on."

It's funny. If these guys were such great leaders and such gritty players, why were they available in the first place? One of those "leaders," Fitzgerald, gave credit back to the front office. "They had a goal in mind to go a certain direction, maybe learning from the other expansion teams, Ottawa and San Jose and

 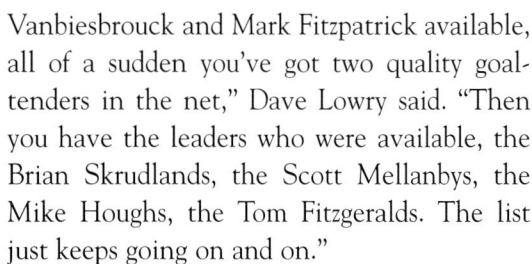
The first chance to view the Panthers came in an exhibition game in Tampa (above). The Panthers lost, but it was very obvious very early that these Cats would be tough to declaw.

Tampa Bay, that we need some character guys," he said. "Not that there weren't character guys on those teams.

"The expansion Florida Panthers get to bare their teeth to the NHL for the first time ..."

"But from day one in the opening meeting in training camp, Bobby Clarke said, 'We're here to win. We're not here to be an expansion team. We're not here to take our lumps and win an occasional game. We're here to compete every night, and if we compete, we can win some games.'"

That approach was evident to those beyond the organization as well. Stu Barnes, who was traded for in November of the first season, was pleased to join the organization because of their approach. "I was actually down here with Winnipeg in October, about three weeks before I got traded. Even at that point, it was only three weeks into the season, and they already had established themselves as one of the hardest-working teams in the league. So when I did get the phone call telling me I got traded, I was pretty excited."

Six days after the inaugural training camp opened, the Panthers took the ice for their first exhibition game. It was only appropriate that it was against the long-time rivals the Tampa Bay Lightning. Okay, this was the first time the two teams met, but remember the first salvo was fired the day the franchise was awarded.

The first three games were against the Lightning, and the Panthers dropped two of the three. They lost the opener in Lakeland but the product was finally on the ice. "It was real exciting," Huizenga said. "You know, exhibition games are exhibition games. But it's always special to watch a team come out for the first time. Everything you do is a first."

The second game was in Jacksonville and the Panthers notched a 5-1 victory. "It's important that you get a taste of winning in the lock-er room when you're a new franchise," Fitzpatrick said. "Even though it's exhibition, it's important to do well."

The Panthers lost their preseason home open-er, again to Tampa Bay, before back-to-back victo-ries over Hartford and Ottawa. They played eight games overall during that first exhibition season, finishing 3-5-0. While they may have impressed each other, they didn't impress the press.

The 1993-94 *Hockey Yearbook* had this to say in its preview of the Panthers: "The expansion Florida Panthers get to bare their teeth to the NHL for the first time in 1993-94. As with any expansion team, expect them to be declawed on many evenings....What's in store for the Panthers in their inaugural season? Look for them to play tough under Neilson's defensive system. If Florida can get some quality defensive help and a proven goalscorer or two, the Panthers can rise in a few short years. In the interim, they will occupy the cellar of the Atlantic Division."

The Sporting News was not nearly so nice. "If Florida's goaltending takes a tumble, the Panthers could be following Ottawa's footsteps in a chase for Washington's dubious expansion record of 8-67-5 in 1974-75. But that shouldn't happen. What should happen, however, is enough stumbling to get Florida the first pick of the 1994 entry draft."

Of course, finagling, not stumbling, already had secured that draft position for the Panthers. But how could the media be so wrong? "The media did not recognize the chemistry we would have, but then, neither did we," Neilson said. "We had no way of knowing how good we were going to be."

The prognosis was improved considerably two days before the season opener when Niedermayer came to terms after a prolonged negotiation. Midnight on October 4 was the deadline for the two sides to come to an agreement or Niedermayer would not be able to play in the

NHL during the 1993-94 season. The morning of the 4th came, and talks were at an "impasse," according to the Fort Lauderdale *Sun-Sentinel.*

"Clarke and (Niedermayer's agent Michael) Barnett said they will speak again today, but both said they are pessimistic," the paper reported in its October 4 issue. But "minutes before the NHL's signing deadline for rookies" the two sides agreed to terms, the *Sun-Sentinel* reported the next day.

"It's a very good deal for both sides. We're glad it's done," Clarke said.

Niedermayer's father, who had gone through the same process two years earlier with older son, Scott, said, "To us it seems like an unbelievable deal."

Niedermayer arrived back in Fort Lauderdale shortly after 8 a.m. on Tuesday, October 5, on a cross-country flight from Los Angeles. After practice at 11 a.m., he got on board a plane bound for Chicago for the regular-season opener.

Once they were in Chicago, Huizenga and the team employees finally got to see the fruit of their labors. Game time approached, and the Blackhawks' front office made sure it was an enjoyable evening.

"Bill Wirtz (Blackhawks owner) was real nice to us," Huizenga said. "He's seen guys like me come and go before, so he went out of his way to make it a pleasant experience. He brought us into his VIP room and let me invite 20 or 25 friends from the Chicago area, because that's where I grew up."

Huizenga, too, went out of his way to make the occasion special. He flew most of the staff from Fort Lauderdale to Chicago to witness the game in person. And while Michael Jordan's retirement stole some of the thunder from a national (and regional in Chicago) perspective, the moment Huizenga, Clarke, Torrey, Neilson and everyone associated with hockey in South Florida had anticipated finally had arrived.

Game On!

Though it took less than a year to create a franchise, Huizenga and the Florida Panthers were ready to kick off their inaugural season, but not before he welcomed the sellout crowd.

TWO

Allll the hoopla was history. All the market surveys were put in boxes. All the preparations had been made. All the exhibition games were played. In a sense, the dues had been paid. It was time to watch the Florida Panthers take to the ice for the first time that really mattered.

October 6, 1993. The Panthers opened their 1993-94 season, and their existence, at storied Chicago Stadium against the Chicago Blackhawks, one of the "original six" of the National Hockey League. The local media knew, or at least believed, that it would be a long season for the Panthers. Expansion teams are supposed to lose a lot. The Panthers had no big goal-scorers, except for freshly signed Rob Niedermayer, and there was no guarantee that his junior numbers would convert to the NHL. The prevailing thought had the Panthers' only hope being John Vanbiesbrouck turning in stellar efforts in goal every once in a while to claim a victory.

This team of leftovers, has-beens and aren't-yets had no chance for success on the season, and the first example of that would be opening night in Chicago.

"Neilson has kept his system simple: Be tough, win faceoffs, make them pay for every goal. At 59, he has the opportunity to craft this team precisely as he wants it," wrote S.L. Price of the *Miami Herald*. Then he added, "He also will be lucky to win 15 games."

Craig Dolch of the *Palm Beach Post* wrote, "Tonight (Wayne Huizenga) will watch the Panthers start paying their dues. So forgive the Panthers if they're not in a festive mood as they prepare for the their regular-season game against the Chicago Blackhawks....Then again, maybe the Panthers should do their celebrating before the game, because they probably won't get much of a chance to afterward."

These guys cover the Panthers!

Fortunately, the players and coaches were too busy to read the papers. They had a game to play. Would their own expectations of being a tough, gritty team that stressed defense and therefore would be in every game come true? Or would the "experts" who predicted the cellar be more accurate? According to Greg Bouris, the Panthers' former director of public and media relations, nobody on the team was looking at the long term that night. They were going through their game-day routine, as if they had done it a thousand times before.

"You're so caught up in the game-day preparations, you don't have that sense of history," he said. "When you reflect back, you have a different feeling, but when you're going through it, it's just part of business. Because I had been in the business for 10 years or so during that time, it seemed like game day for any established team. The players felt the same way, but everybody knew this was special. This was our coming-out party."

And they came out hot. If a tie is like kissing your sister, these guys didn't mind at all puckering up for "sis." The Panthers tied the Blackhawks, 4-4, and earned the first point in team history. "What a great way to start the season," Huizenga said after the game. "These guys played much better than I thought they would. They played beyond my wildest expectations."

First-year, not expansion

The Panthers did not play like a typical expansion team in their first season. In fact, they compiled the best first-year record in professional sports history for a team in a non-expansion division, 33-34-17 (.494 winning percentage), and fell just short of a playoff spot.

Huizenga toured the visitors' clubhouse congratulating each of his players following the tie. "Wayne was going up to everybody saying, 'Nice win. Way to come up here and win,'" Bouris said. "Even though we tied the game, it was like a major victory to go into Chicago Stadium and not be out of place at all."

Back to the details. Rob Niedermayer, Evgeny Davydov and Scott Mellanby are three names that will stay in the Panthers record book forever. Niedermayer and Davydov earned the assists while Mellanby notched the first goal in team history at the 12:31 mark of the first period.

"A lot of people won't remember that, but it is special for me," Mellanby said. "It's certainly

> ## "What a great way to start the season ... these guys played beyond my wildest expectations."

something I will remember for a long time."

The Panthers led, 1-0, after one period, but Chris Chelios scored twice in the second period to give the Blackhawks the lead heading into the third period. But the close, low-scoring game turned wide open in the third period. First, Gord Murphy tied the game at 5:18 of the period on a slap shot that he was "hoping would go in." "I had a good clear lane to the net and was just hoping it would hit one of our sticks," he said.

Twenty-eight seconds later, with the Blackhawks on a power-play because of a Murphy slashing penalty, Jeremy Roenick tapped in a rebound in front of the net to give the Blackhawks the 3-2 lead. That lead lasted just 3:04 because Andrei Lomakin deked Ed Belfour on a breakaway and knotted the game once again.

The Panthers regained the lead with 6:20 remaining. Brian Skrudland passed to Scott

Levins in front of the net and the puck ended back on Skrudland's stick. He poked it past Belfour to give the Panthers the 4-3 advantage. The Blackhawks had lost their season opener the previous season to a first-year team from Florida (Tampa Bay), and they weren't about to let the same thing happen.

Roenick blasted a 40-footer past Vanbiesbrouck with 3:53 left to tie the game at 4-4. The Panthers had acquitted themselves very well. Each of the four Blackhawks goals was scored on the power play, after the Panthers had killed five such Chicago opportunities in the first period. And while they couldn't claim the win, they certainly claimed victory.

"The important thing is we won," Niedermayer said. "I mean we tied."

Clarke summarized the feelings of the organization. "If it weren't for the power play, we would've beaten them," he said. "It's the first game, so there's a lot of emotion on both sides. In a couple of weeks, things will settle out and we'll see where we are. But what we asked of the club, they did. They worked hard, listened to the coaches. They did real (well)."

One of the most difficult aspects of professional sports is playing games on back-to-back nights. The night after the emotional opener against Chicago, the Panthers had to lace up the skates again to take on St. Louis, again on the road. The Panthers played tough for two periods, and trailed just 2-1 heading into the third period. But a tired Panthers team gave up three third-period goals to a Blues team that was opening its season, and the first loss in team history was hung on the board, to the tune of 5-3.

Let's see. A tie and a loss. As the Panthers headed into their third game, there was but one

result left to taste. Once again, there was extra drama surrounding this one. The game was at Tampa Bay, the Panthers' natural rival. The Lightning were one year removed from their inaugural season and were in no mood to let the Panthers upstage their home opener in the ThunderDome. An NHL regular-season attendance record was expected. And Wayne Huizenga was there.

Remember how the residents of Tampa felt about Huizenga? There were advertisements that warned of the visit by "Wayne Huizenga's Panthers from Miami." A sign hung from the balcony that read, "Make Wayne Huizenga and the Panthers extinct."

But much to the chagrin of the Lightning fans, Huizenga was not on the ice. Much to the delight of the Panthers fans, John Vanbiesbrouck was. The Beezer stopped all 36 Tampa Bay shots and the Panthers had their first win and first shutout, 2-0. Scott

Scott Mellanby (left and above) was an offensive threat from the beginning for the Panthers. He scored the first goal in team history and led the team in goals (30) and points (60) for the first season. If the puck was in front of the net, usually so was Mellanby.

Levins scored a power-play goal at the 2:19 mark of the second period and Tom Fitzgerald added an open-net goal with 27 seconds left in the game.

When the microphone went dead, it was time for Huizenga ... to do his best stand-up routine.

Vanbiesbrouck shone all game long. The Lightning outshot the Panthers, 17-4, in the first period, but none of Tampa's shots could get in. In the third period, with the Panthers clinging to a 1-0 lead, Vanbiesbrouck stopped a three-on-none rush. He knocked the puck off of the stick of Petr Klima before Klima could get off a decent shot. Then, when John Tucker sent the rebound back to Klima, Vanbiesbrouck deflected the shot into the crowd.

"I don't care as much about the shutout as I do getting that first win," Vanbiesbrouck said. "You never know how long that is going to take." It was just a matter of time with Vanbiesbrouck in the pipes. "The way John was playing, they wouldn't have gotten one past him if we had played seven periods," Neilson added. "He made it look easy."

The record crowd came as expected. Surpassing the previous record by more than 6,000 fans, the Panthers and Lightning played before 27,227 people, most of them charged up about the Lightning. "I don't mind sending 27,000 people home miserable," Neilson said.

33443

Home is where the Panthers found themselves after the three-game trip to start the season. A 1-1-1 record was nothing to be ashamed of, and the team had proven it would not be easy fodder for anybody. That was comforting, as the opponent for the first-ever home opener was the Pittsburgh Penguins, one year removed from back-to-back Stanley Cup championships.

Edwin Pope of *The Miami Herald* wrote, "(The fans) went so bananas for souvenirs that the ATM lines were as long as the lines at the souvenir stands."

The Panthers did not disappoint the fans either. Two fluke goals were all that kept the Cats from their second straight shutout and second straight win. Martin Straka, who was signed by the Panthers during the 1995-96 sea-

"The crowd was great. The excitement and the enthusiasm were terrific," Huizenga said. "Even though the microphone didn't work well, it was a fun night."

The pregame show was flashy. There was a laser show, a fireworks show and ice dancers. But when the microphone went dead, it was time for Huizenga, chairman of Blockbuster *Entertainment*, to do his best stand-up routine. "Like all new toys, batteries are extra," he said, and then introduced Dean Jordan as the "vice president in charge of microphones." Still, the crowd came away from the arena in love with the glitz of the NHL.

son, scored the first goal in Miami Arena when he dribbled one past Vanbiesbrouck at 17:40 of the second period. The Beezer seemed to stop the shot, but after it hit the ice, it rolled into the net. Then, in the third period, Vanbiesbrouck left the crease to try and clear the puck from his zone. But Joe Mullen deflected the pass and then fired it into the net to give the Penguins a 2-0 lead.

Mellanby scored his third goal of the season, and the Panthers' first home goal, at the 11:32 mark of the third to bring the Panthers to

(Top left) Once the team was assembled, it was time for (standing from left: Huizenga, Torrey and Clarke) to watch their team in action. (Left) Huizenga welcomed commissioner Gary Bettman (third from left) and a sell-out crowd to the first home game. (Above) The Panthers' first win was a 2-0 shutout that came at the home of in-state rival Tampa Bay.

within one goal. But they could not score again. "We all felt on the bench that we would tie it up (after Mellanby's goal)," Neilson said.

"If you think you're going to come in here and steal points, you're not going to," Pittsburgh coach Ed Johnston said.

That was quite a comment from the coach of one of the '90s best teams. "With the superstars they have on their roster and the high-powered talent they have, that was a big game for us," Bouris said. "The media was out in full force. There was an average of five writers assigned by the three major daily papers here, *The Miami Herald*, *The Sun-Sentinal* and *The Palm Beach Post*. Every television station, including the two hispanic stations, was going live from the building. We had English and Spanish radio play-by-play ready to do the game. All the hype and hoopla was special.

> ## "(The fans) went so bananas for souvenirs that the ATM lines were as long as the lines at the souvenir stands."

"This was it. That was the real opener, in the minds of a lot of people in south Florida, anyway, because this was our home opener. We lost the game, but nonetheless, we were a franchise now. We got it out of the way and we were ready to go."

Actually, the one-goal loss to the Penguins was emblematic of the 1993-94 season. The Panthers were in almost every game, losing by more than three goals only three times. They

hovered around the .500 mark for much of the year, finishing one game under the break-even mark. They also scored the exact same number of goals (233) as they gave up.

Those statistics meant it was time for a win. The Panthers came into their fifth game with a 1-2-1 record, and though they only had the one game, they had not treated the home fans to a victory. The Ottawa Senators were next

Angeles Kings came into Miami for the first time. The Panthers shut down Gretzky, but the Kings escaped with a 2-2 tie. Jesse Belanger, who had scored his first NHL goal in the previous game, and Gord Murphy scored for the Panthers, who established a team record with 52 shots on goal.

The Panthers went 3-4-1 over the next eight games before heading to hallowed

on the docket, two nights after the Penguins. Rob Niedermayer scored the first goal of his NHL career and Scott Levins became the first Panther to score two goals in a game as the Panthers downed the Senators, 5-4.

Two straight ties followed the Senators game. First, the Lightning overcame a 3-1 deficit to earn a 3-3 tie. Then Wayne Gretzky and the Los

Montreal Forum for a match-up with the Stanley Cup champion Canadiens. As was true almost every night, this game was special for at least one of the Panthers. With practically everybody on the team having been unprotected by another NHL team, every night was

Whether it was standing in line to buy souvenirs (top left) or just standing to cheer a great play (left), Panthers fans quickly adopted this new team. The Pittsburgh Penguins escaped with a 2-1 victory, plus respect for the new team, in the Panthers' home opener (top).

"Revenge Night" for somebody. Against the Canadiens, it was Brian Skrudland's and Jesse Belanger's turns to prove that their former team was wrong.

"The biggest thing for me was winning in the Montreal Forum," Skrudland said when asked for a favorite memory during the first three years. "A lot of the guys said they had never done that before. For me, going back as an ex-Canadien and winning was a big deal."

"For the most part, no matter where we went, we had a player on our team that played for that team," Bouris said. "Whether he was released during the expansion draft or traded just prior to the expansion draft, when we went into a city, or when a team came to play us,

"We're going to show them."

there was somebody in our locker room who had been 'slighted' by that franchise. So there was a rallying cry from his teammates, 'Hey, we're playing Montreal tonight and Skrudland used to play for Montreal. Let's show them they made a mistake.'

"It wasn't Brian Skrudland saying this. It was all his teammates saying, 'We're going to show them.' In Quebec, it was 'Let's do it for Billy Lindsay.' The Islanders? 'OK, Mark Fitzpatrick, you're playing in goal, Tom Fitzgerald, it's your night.' Boom, we're fired up. The guys wanted to show these teams they made big mistakes.

"Every guy could identify, because they were all in the same position. And that was a huge motivating factor that lasted throughout the first year, and still is there, I'm sure. They all learned about teamwork by playing that way. That's not to say they didn't know about it before, but they learned about cohesiveness, they learned about playing defensively, they learned about playing for 60 minutes, playing as hard as you can."

The Panthers went into the Forum and stopped the defending champs, 3-1. Belanger, Niedermayer and Randy Gilhen scored for the Panthers, who let it be known that history be darned, there was no team that could intimidate these Cats.

but a thrill. All of a sudden, I was a big part of a team. Here, everybody plays and everybody contributes. Everyone here has been in a situation where they were the odd man out. When they're put into a situation where they're counted on night in and night out, I think that's one of the reasons we've been so successful."

Another piece to the puzzle was added in late November, when the Panthers sent Gilhen and a fourth-round pick to Winnipeg for Stu Barnes and a sixth-round pick. "Things were not working out for me in Winnipeg," said Barnes, who had been the Jets' first-round choice (fourth overall) in 1989. "When I did get a chance to come to Florida to play, it was not only a relief,

It's interesting that the Panthers have had so much success with "cast-offs," while the other expansion teams have struggled. It goes back to that character issue. The Panthers drafted and signed players who were not afraid to work. There may not have been many superstars in the bunch, but no one was allowed to slough off.

Championship teams are built on defense and goaltending. The Panthers were blessed with two quality goaltenders. Having Fitzpatrick (left) within reach made it easier to give Vanbiesbrouck a rest. (Above) Niedermayer found the going tough in his first season.

Bill Torrey

In a recent *Blondie* comic strip, Dagwood Bumstead went to work one day without his trademark bow tie. Nobody recognized him. There's no word whether anyone would recognize Panthers' president Bill Torrey without his bow tie, maybe because he's never been seen without it.

Okay, that's a bit of a stretch. But the only thing that is more closely associated with Torrey than his neckware is the fact that he knows how to build a winning hockey team.

Torrey is best known for his construction of the four-time Stanley Cup champion New York Islanders. But the method he used in the early 1970s with the Islanders is the same formula he used with the Florida Panthers 20 years later, and the early returns indicate he's riding another winner.

"This team is solid because it has a solid foundation," said Denis Potvin, a member of the four Islanders championship teams and the television analyst for the Panthers. "They didn't start by trying to appease the media, by drafting big-name players. They've had a couple of summers where they could have gone into the free-agency and gotten big name players to fill seats like so many teams have. But it's never been Torrey's way to do that. He would rather develop young players and have them be long-term stars. If you can have a player for three or four years, and develop him, the fan is going to relate to him a lot more than the traveling mercenary, doing a job for a year then moving on to another team."

Torrey's plan with the Panthers and the Islanders is not much different than it would be if he were building a football team. Or a basketball team. Or a team for virtually any team sport. The theory? Defense wins championships.

"No matter how good your goaltending is, if you're giving up 40 to 50 shots a night, you're not going to win," Torrey said. "If you look back over history, the teams that were successful for any period of time all had better defense than anybody else."

The other ingredient in the team-building formula is character. The Islanders, who had superstars like Mike Bossy and Bryan Trottier, also had role players like Clark Gillies, Butch Goring and Ken Morrow. They all worked together to form a cohesive unit that resulted in hoisting Lord Stanley's Cup four consecutive years. The Panthers are following the blueprint exactly. The Islanders missed the playoffs their first two years, though they were a lot farther than one point out. In their third season, the Isles made the conference finals, but lost, the same position they earned in the fourth year.

The Islanders won the Cup in their eighth year of existence, which would be the 2000-2001 year for the Panthers. But Torrey is not willing to wait that long. With free agency and player movement much friendlier, he can acquire the talent to produce the results in a shorter span. And he, like owner Wayne Huizenga, allows the people under him to do their jobs without him looking over their shoulders.

"He allows you to do what you want to do," general manager Bryan Murray said. "We talk about some of the decisions that have to be made, but he allows you to do it. I think that is critical if you're going to try to build a program."

That even goes as far as building a franchise from a public relations standpoint. "The guy is a legend," said goaltender John Vanbiesbrouck, who played against Torrey's Islanders teams as a member of the New York Rangers. "I like to be compared to those Islanders teams. The difference is that we had to turn this area into a hockey environment when nobody thought it could be. It is now and that stands alone. He's a great delegator. He lets (executive vice president and alternate governor) Dean Jordan and (vice president of marketing) Declan Bolger do their jobs of promoting the team."

Even Torrey's competitors in hockey have great respect for him. Murray recalled his first encounter with Torrey when he was in his first year as coach of the Washington Capitals. "They beat us the first game, 5-3, and Bill was one of the few guys who came over to speak to me," he said. "He told me, 'Hey, Kid, get your team to play like that every night, and you're going to win a lot of games in this league.'

"Bill is a gentleman. He's a knowledgeable guy. He's a hockey man. We also communicate well. When Bill first approached me about coming here, certainly one of the decisions was the people you work with, and that is a real legitimate reason why I came here. "

The reason Torrey is in South Florida is his respect for Huizenga, and the urge to prove one more time that he could get it done.

"You don't get many opportunities like this, I don't think I've reached that stage where I just want to sit in an easy chair," he said. "The game means a lot to me, it always has. It's been a part of my life since I can remember, growing up in Montreal. When Mr. Huizenga first talked to me, I was first of all drawn to him as a person. He's a very interesting, amazing person.

"Second, to build a team from scratch again, and to be involved in building an arena from scratch, that kind of caught my interest, and certainly I haven't regretted it. It's been a great thing. Just the excitement of seeing it done; a lot of people didn't feel that hockey could work down here. I felt like it would be very successful here with the right team and with Wayne's ability to promote, and the excitement he creates.

"When I left the Island, I had a lot of other things to think about. I knew expansion was coming. I talked to some other teams about doing some things, but once I really started talking with Wayne, nothing else really interested me."

His bow tie still is knotted, because he's still hard at work. He's built the Panthers into one of the league's elite teams, and he won't stop working until they're at the top.

And just like Dagwood Bumstead when he is constructing one of his famous sandwiches, Torrey never bites off more than he can chew.

●

Torrey had nothing left to prove in hockey. He could have retired his bow tie, but he chose to give it another shot and helped build the Panthers into a championship-caliber team.

T he first test of how that theory was working arrived with a game at Anaheim on December 7. The Ducks, of course, had gone through the drafts and entered the league at the same time as the Panthers. Comparing apples with apples finally was possible, and the Panthers turned up golden and delicious.

Comparing apples with apples ... the Panthers turned up golden and delicious.

For the third time in four games, Scott Mellanby scored the Panthers' first goal of the game. Belanger added a goal and Greg Hawgood scored the game-winner. Vanbiesbrouck stopped 28 of 30 shots, as the Panthers edged the Ducks, 3-2.

It was satisfying for the players and the front office. It was the first sign of the excellence in player procurement, that still is evident in the fourth season. "Anaheim had a good draft as well," assistant general manager Chuck Fletcher said. "They got some key players on their team from that draft, including Guy Hebert as their number one goalie, and Bobby Dollas, who is their assistant captain and one of their top defensemen. They were able to get some quality players, but at this point in time, it certainly appears that we were able to draft more NHL players.

"We still have many of our players almost from the opening night. That's a credit to the players as much as to the organization, because when we picked up these players, most of them were coming off poor seasons or injury-prone seasons, and that's why they were made available to us. They turned their careers around and worked hard.

"Very few teams have as many guys from four years ago as we do, and that's a credit to both Bob Clarke and Bryan Murray. People look at and judge the general magager by the trades he makes. I've always said that you have to judge a general manager by the trades he doesn't make. We've turned down a lot of opportunities to move some key players who are part of this team right now. A lot of teams have wanted John Vanbiesbrouck and Brian Skrudland and Scott Mellanby. We've resisted a lot of tempting offers for draft picks and young players. We've done it because we want to build consistency. We like that the players know each other. We have a tremendous chemistry, and we're very hesitant to break that up.

"Bryan and Bob have done an unbelievable job, because the trades we have made have added key ingredidients to the team's scoring with Barnes and with (Ray) Sheppard. We picked up (Robert) Svehla, who is an unbelievable defenseman. We signed Terry Carkner for nothing (in compensation). These are key players on our team. These players, without really giving up very much, have been the key. We haven't had to trade any of our veteran leadership at all."

That veteran leadership was put to the test three days before Christmas as the New York Rangers came to town. A Miami Arena-record of 14,706 saw former Ranger Vanbiesbrouck stop 33 New York shots en route to a 3-2 victory over the Blue Shirts. It was the first victory over the Rangers for Beezer, Neilson and the rest of the Panthers.

The Panthers followed that win with a win at Tampa Bay, a tie at Washington and a win at Hartford to close the 1993 portion of the schedule with a 15-15-6 record. It was the first time since November 10 (7-7-3) that the team was at .500. The victory over Hartford also gave Florida a chance to be above .500 for the first time in history with a victory against Anaheim. Four Panthers scored goals and Vanbiesbrouck made 37 saves as the Panthers defeated Anaheim, 4-2, despite being outshot, 39-19. The win gave the Panthers a 2-0 sweep of their fellow first-year team.

A rematch with the Rangers followed that

 Veterans like Mellanby (top left), Murphy (left) and Lowry (above, left) were critical in the development of the Panthers' young stars like Niedermayer (above, right).

Vanbiesbrouck made a team-record 51 saves against his former teammates.

game. It was a big moment for the former Rangers, because the game was played at Madison Square Garden in New York. Vanbiesbrouck drew a long ovation from the Rangers fans as he led his team onto the ice. "BEEZER, BEEZER," the crowd chanted at their former netminder.

"They supported me for a long time," he said. "I'm sure they'll continue to support me. I love playing in New York. It's a great place to play. The 10 years I spent here were fun. I thought we had a chance to come out of this game with something. We got nothing."

The Panthers lost to the Rangers, 3-2. But Vanbiesbrouck certainly did his part to assure a victory. He made a team-record 51 saves in the contest. "You can rely on a goalie for a while, but this has got to stop somewhere," Skrudland said after the game. "We're allowing far too many shots. There

have been far too many games with 45 or 50 shots lately."

Vanbiesbrouck earned the second star for the game, but the Panthers fell back to .500. A 4-1 loss to the Devils four nights later dropped them under .500, but then a 5-0-4 stretch over the next nine games put the Panthers in the thick of the playoff race.

One of the keys to that run was the acquisition of Bob Kudelski from Ottawa. The Panthers sent Levins and Davydov to the Senators in exchange for Kudelski. He already had been selected to the all-star game in New York, where he would join Vanbiesbrouck in representing the Panthers. Kudelski scored four goals during the unbeaten stretch, including two against the Capitals. He also scored two goals in

the all-star game, and Vanbiesbrouck was the winning goalie.

While the unbeaten stretch was nothing to sneeze at, the fact that two of the games were against the defending-champion Canadiens made it even more impressive. The first match-up was in Montreal and five Panthers (Mellanby, Kudelski, Lomakin, Hough and Fitzgerald) scored as the Panthers blitzed the Habs, 5-2. Vanbiesbrouck again was named first star after stopping 43 of 45 Montreal shots.

But the real eye-opener was nine days later when the Canadiens came to Miami for the final game against the Panthers during the season. It was bad enough for the defending league champs to lose to a first-year team, but

Vanbiesbrouck's stellar play (left) made him a fast favorite with the fans who formed the Beezer Brigade (top left). Lowry (above) knew the crease was not a forward-friendly zone, but that never stopped him from venturing in, netting 15 goals and 37 points in 1993-94.

if the Panthers could win or tie, the Canadiens would take a goose-egg into the second season. The Panthers already had defeated Montreal twice on the road, and the two teams had tied in the first meeting at The Miami Arena.

"We have four lines of guys who all feel equally important to the task."

This game was all Florida.

The Panthers scored so many goals, even the mechanical roar from the scoreboard got a raspy voice. Mellanby and Lomakin each tallied two goals, while Hull, Fitzgerald and the two former Canadiens—Skrudland and Belanger—netted one apiece.

We wanted to get the knife in and keep turning it and turning it and turning it," Skrudland said. "Satisfaction isn't a word we like to use around here."

There was no doubt this game was a confidence builder. The Canadiens had had trouble with the Panthers, but they still were the defending champions. With their pride on the line, the visitors from the north never were in the game.

"The Canadiens were the New York Yankees of hockey," Bouris said, "and we had beaten them in a couple of games prior to that. So you know the chip on their shoulder had to be growing, 'How can they do this to us? Enough of this, we've got to put this franchise in its place.'

"We were creating a lot of excitement outside of hockey. We had three big media organizations covering the game that night. *Sports Illustrated* was in to do a feature on us that was our first major feature in that magazine. CNN was here to cover the game for a feature. There was a television network here, too. You couldn't have asked for anything better—wholloping the Montreal Canadiens in front of a sold-out crowd going crazy. To humiliate them like that was really an exclamation point on the season.

"We established a foundation for the franchise that was going to be, 'We're never going to get pushed around. We're always going to be competitive. We may not have as much talent as you do on paper, but we have four lines of guys who all feel equally important to the task.' Because of that, there was a lot of accountability in the dressing room. When they went out to play the games, other teams weren't ready in January to face a team that was that hungry and that fired up for 60 minutes."

stars in more than half of the games in which he played. He was first star 16 times, second star eight times and third star six times in 57 games.

Belanger also made Panthers history following the game by being named the NHL Player of the Week. He was the first Panther to gain the honor and was the first player to earn the award during his team's inaugural season, since the award began in the 1980-81 season. Also, the nine-game unbeaten string was a record for a first-year team in the NHL.

The ninth game of the unbeaten run was in Buffalo. Two familiar names keyed the 3-2 victory for the Panthers. Belanger scored two goals and Vanbiesbrouck recorded 37 saves to earn another first star. Vanbiesbrouck finished the season being named one of the three

January had come to an end, and the Panthers were 21-17-10. They had earned 16 out of a possible 24 points for the month. Six games past the midway point of the season, the

Scoring celebrations (left) were not that common as the Panthers scored just 2.8 goals per game, but an outstanding defense and excellent goaltending kept the opponents from celebrating too often. Niedermayer (above) and Panthers battled in every game.

team had 52 points. Considering the last team to reach the playoffs the previous season had 86 points, the Panthers only needed 34 points in their last 36 games to reach that plateau.

"We're on bit of a mission right now and we want it to continue," Skrudland said. "This could be fun, this second half."

Clarke took the politically correct approach. "We're halfway through the season," he said. "Let's not get ahead of the game. We have to scratch, claw and work each night."

That was the *modus operandi* for the Boston Bruins when they came to Miami February 6.

But that wasn't enough. Fitzpatrick stopped 38 shots. That's out of 38. The Bruins scratched and clawed all evening, but couldn't get the puck past "Fitzy," as he recorded the first home shutout in team history. It was just another example of the value of "the team." While Vanbiesbrouck was the star, without Fitzpatrick, the Panthers would be left with a hole in the net on far too many occasions.

"That's how this team has been successful over the past three or four years," Fitzpatrick said

recently. "Every guy brings something to the table. Obviously, some guys bring a lot more to the table, like Johnny and Brian Skrudland, because they are the guys we count on night

> **"Let's not get ahead of the game. We have to scratch, claw and work each night."**

after night. But it's a total team effort. As long as we've got 20 guys pulling the rope, there is no reason for this team not to be successful."

A week later, after a 2-1 victory over Vancouver, the Panthers were five games over .500, a high-water mark for the season. The Panthers managed a season-low 15 shots, but two got by Kirk McLean. Fitzpatrick was the first star of the game, with 33 saves in 34 shots.

But then the Panthers hit the skids. Eight losses in nine games left the Panthers two games under .500. The first two losses—at Detroit and at Buffalo—were decisive. The Red Wings returned the trip to Miami for the next game and escaped with a 4-3 victory in overtime. The only win during the skid was a 3-2 decision in Winnipeg. Stu Barnes, the former Jet, scored the game-winner for Florida.

Five straight losses to end the nine-game stretch—four of them by one goal and the fifth by two—left the Panthers scurrying for momentum. Once again, Fitzpatrick was the hero as he nearly pitched a shutout in Vancouver. He stopped 34 of 35 shots, and the Panthers escaped with a 2-1 victory. They followed that with a 5-3 win in Edmonton. Before the latest run ended, the Panthers had gone 5-1-3 and were back in contention for a playoff spot.

 The fans enjoyed getting "up close" with the Panthers, whether that means watching Niedermayer (left) "take care of business" or having Lowry (above) sign a souvenir.

On March 8, the Panthers were given permission to do the unfathomable: mail playoff-ticket-order forms to their season-ticket holders. "I think we've had some big wins along the line," Lindsay said. "But halfway through our first year to see that we were in a playoff race was really a telltale story of what kind of guys we had here."

On March 20, the Flyers came into Miami trailing the Panthers by two points for the eighth and final playoff spot. They left trailing by four points. Vanbiesbrouck, who called it "definitely a playoff game," turned back 45 of 48 shots, and the Panthers won, 5-3. "I've been in enough to know that was definitely a playoff game," the Beezer said. "We've been playing playoff hockey all season long."

Vanbiesbrouck fought off a 5-on-3 situation for two minutes in the second period without giving up a goal. "It was Beezer's night," Neilson understated.

"We missed by one point. It really would have been great in our first year to make the playoffs."

With the win, the Panthers tied the Flyers' own first-year (1967-68) records of 73 points and 31 wins (Hartford also recorded 73 points in 1979-80, its first year). The first mark fell the following night by cooling off the New Jersey Devils. The Devils entered the game with an 8-1-1 mark in their last 10 games and had moved to within two points of first place. Dave Lowry scored the tying goal as the Panthers erased a two-goal New Jersey lead.

A tie against Toronto and a loss in Philadelphia left the Panthers perched on 75 points and 31 wins. The victory mark fell when Fitzpatrick stopped his former team, the Islanders, for the third time in the season, as he made 32 saves in a 3-1 victory. Unfortunately, with nine games remaining in the season, the

Panthers only would manage one more victory and four ties. That gave them 83 points, when 84 was required.

"I thought it was great," Huizenga said of the playoff push. "I was sitting on the edge of the chair all the time, saying, 'We've got to win this game.' We missed by one point. My goodness, somewhere along the way we needed one more tie. It really would have been great in our first year to make the playoffs, but it wasn't meant to be."

Somewhere along the way, something did happen. Huizenga became a hockey fan. "Oh yes, hockey is fantastic."

Much of the credit for converting Huizenga, and thousands of his friends, has to go to Neilson. His team was in nearly every game. Fans knew when they came to a game they were in store for a barn-burner because the Panthers played hard every minute of every game. And the Panthers themselves give Neilson credit.

"Roger was the perfect coach for our first couple of years," Lowry said. "He was not a yeller or a screamer. He's a great student of the game. He knows the game extremely well and he gave us a system to play with. He wanted to make sure the guys knew how to play on their own end. That's what kept us in the games. We may not have scored a lot of goals, but the other team had to fight for everything they got."

Despite the late swoon, the Panthers had their playoff chances in their own hands. They trailed the Islanders, the team that probably would be the final hurdle, by one point with each team having two games remaining. The Islanders played at Tampa Bay and then in Miami, while the Panthers hosted their last two games. Wins in both would give them a berth in the postseason. A tie and an Islanders tie or loss at Tampa would make

the final game for all the marbles. There were other chances, too, but the penultimate game against Quebec would set the stage.

Neilson said before that game that he would not settle for a tie because of the playoff ramifications. If the score was tied in the final minutes, the coach said he would pull his goalie. He did that, but it wasn't because the score was tied in the final minute. Vanbiesbrouck gave up three goals in the first 30 minutes of the game and was yanked. It was the first time all season that the Beezer had been pulled because of ineffectiveness. "It happens in all goal-

tenders' careers," he said. "It's a very empty feeling to let your teammates down."

That left the Panthers rooting hard for...TAMPA BAY! The Lightning had to defeat the Islanders for the Panthers to have any chance at a playoff spot. It was difficult to muster, but the

"Not on my ice," Fitzpatrick seems to be saying to the New Jersey Devils (left). Panthers frenzy transcended all sports in South Florida. (Above) Dolphins' coach Don Shula enjoys the action with Huizenga, while the fans around them focus on the action on the ice.

fans in South Florida had to become fans of the team from the left coast of Florida.

"They have been playing well lately," Neilson said. "They could come up big tonight."

There was some thinking that the Lightning might not try real hard in the game because it would help their hated rivals if they won. Torrey even was misquoted in the New York Post, saying he called NHL commissioner Gary Bettman to ask him to make sure the

"You're saying a professional team would roll over?" Vanbiesbrouck asked rhetorically. "They have a lot of pride. I think they'll have too much pride to roll over."

The Lightning didn't roll over, but they didn't win, either. "I don't think we could do anything but give Tampa Bay major credit," Bouris said. "(Daren) Puppa played great. The whole team played great. But in the end, the Islanders beat them to clinch that spot."

Lightning didn't tank it. Balderdash. Torrey said he called Bettman, but mostly to talk about collective bargaining and the draft. When he was asked if he had discussed the subject of "tanking" with Bettman, he jokingly said he would be concerned only if the Lightning called up a goaltender from its International Hockey League affiliate.

The players were even more incredulous.

New York's victory made the last game meaningless, at least in terms of the playoffs. "I don't think the schedule-maker ever thought a game between the first-year Panthers and the Islanders, who had made the conference semifinals the previous year, would mean the last playoff spot," Bouris said. "Even though the game was meaningless in a hockey sense, it was special night for us.

"To this day, we've played a lot of special games, but I don't think that any one is more special to everybody—because I don't think we knew what to expect—than our 'Fan Appreciation Night,' our day to give back a little something."

The first thing the Panthers gave was a superb effort in the game. Vanbiesbrouck came right back after his poor showing against Quebec and stopped 25 of 26 shots. He even

short speech, thanking the fans for their support. "We were hoping a few people would stay in the stands, and we would end the season and go our way," Bouris said. "With five or 10 minutes to go, a fan had a sign that stretched across two sections of Miami Arena and

"I know I had to do everything I could not to shed a tear. It was that emotional."

stopped the first penalty shot against the Panthers in their history, stoning Zigmund Palffy on a split save. Mellanby scored his 30th goal of the season and the Panthers won, 4-1.

After the game, the players were supposed to stick around and toss T-shirts into the crowd. Skrudland, the captain, was supposed to make a

unfurled it behind our bench area. It said something like, 'We love you, Panthers,' and it was signed, it seemed, by almost every fan in attendance. When they stood up with the banner, the rest of the crowd just stood up and

Spreading across more sections that the camera could capture, the fans' sign ("Thank you, Panthers"), not to mention thousands of signatures, displayed at the end of the 1993-94 season (left) showed the Panthers how they felt. The feeling certainly was mutual (above).

gave the team a standing ovation for the rest of the game."

When the game ended, the post-game celebration began. Where it would end was anybody's guess. Skrudland told the fans that the players felt they had the best fans in the NHL. Skrudland choked back the tears, and he wasn't the only one.

"I know I had to do everything I could not to shed a tear. It was that emotional," Bouris said. "It was amazing to see the players choking back their emotions. I don't think Brian was blowing smoke. I think he meant it from the heart. These fans overnight became the best, most loyal, most supportive group going. Although it was 'Fan Appreciation Night,' they ended up taking control, and it was 'Panther Appreciation Night.'"

If there was anybody connected with the team that wasn't choked up by this point, they soon would be. After dispensing the T-shirts, the players, one by one and on their own, skated over to the section that Wayne Huizenga occupied, and gave him a thumbs-up. "It was their way to say 'Way-to-go, thanks for bringing us here. Thanks for bringing hockey here. Look what you've done. Look at the people you've touched.' He was so touched by the players spontaneously going over there that even he was moved to tears," Bouris said.

More than three years later, Huizenga's thoughts about that night haven't changed. "Oh boy, I get choked up just thinking about it now," he said.

"I'll never forget that game. It was unbelievable. Everybody knew we were out of the playoffs, and the team that beat us out was the Islanders. We won that game big-time, and the fans went wild. After the game, the fans

just hung around. The players threw stuff and signed their names, and the fans just stayed. Nobody left.

"We lost a lot of money that first year, but it was still worth it. It was a great, great night. The fans were great. But the players were what made the fans great."

The first season was history. The Panthers missed the playoffs by one agonizing point. But there was reason to celebrate. And anticipate. The team had established records for wins (33, tied with Anaheim, who had 71 points) and points (83) for a first-year NHL team. Even more impressive, they achieved the best won-lost percentage (.494) for a first-year franchise in professional sports history.

Vanbiesbrouck was a finalist for the Vezina Trophy for the league's best goaltender (he finished second) and the Hart Trophy as the league's most valuable player (fourth). Skrudland was named a finalist for the Selke Trophy for the league's best defensive forward (third).

The future was so bright, the Panthers had to wear shades.

The future was so bright, the Panthers had to wear shades.

The Panthers fell one point short of a playoff spot, but the season was not without honor, both literally and figuratively, for the team. Vanbiesbrouck and Kudelski (left) represented the team at the all-star game, and the Beezer (above) was a finalist for the Vezina Trophy.

The *expectations* surrounding most second-year teams are not that high. But then again, the 1994-95 Florida Panthers were not most second-year teams. They had just come off the most successful first year in professional sports history. They had missed the playoffs by one point. They were *this close*!

They had played outstanding defense during the first year, giving up just 2.8 goals per game. If they could figure out how to get more goals on offense (that 2.8 figure is the same for the offense, which isn't outstanding), then a playoff berth definitely was within reach.

However, that reach was dealt its first forearm shiver on June 15 when Bob Clarke left the team to return to Philadelphia. Clarke, who had played his entire 15-year career for the Flyers, and had had two previous stints in the front office of the team, said it was not an easy decision. But it was the right one.

"(Leaving after one year) wasn't something that was planned when I went to Florida," he said. "I sold my house in Philly and I enrolled my kids in school. We were going to stay. I ended up thinking that the Panthers really didn't need Bob Clarke and Bill Torrey in the same organization. I think there was a crossover a lot of times between Bill and me.

"I loved Mr. Huizenga, and he treated my family and me really well. But Mr. (Ed) Snider (Flyers' majority owner) was also someone who was obviously a very good friend of mine. He offered me team ownership and different and more responsibilities—a lot of things that Florida couldn't provide for me and didn't need to. It was a chance to come back to what was home for my children.

"It wasn't easy to make the decision to leave the Panthers. The Panthers were special to me and my family. But when you're in a position like I was in, and you've got somebody saying, 'You can come back and have some team ownership,' and it's a team that obviously I love, I had to take it. I was being offered what no general manager has ever been offered, and it was from a man who was almost like a father to me."

Huizenga understood Clarke's decision to leave, but he didn't like it. "He's a good guy, I liked Bobby a lot," Huizenga said. "I hated to see him go. I hoped that he would have stayed. He got pulled away by Snider. Actually, Snider stole Bobby; tampered with him and stole him. It wasn't fair the way they treated us."

The first year had brought a strange combination at the helm of the Panthers. A former Islander (Torrey), a former Flyer (Clarke) and a former Ranger (Neilson) worked together to achieve the previously mentioned success. Now that was done. It would be a month and a half before a successor was named. But there was work to be done.

The amateur draft that had brought the Panthers Rob Niedermayer the previous year was coming. This year the team would have the first pick. Recall that in 1993 the Panthers had a choice of going first (among the two expansion teams,

The season that left us short

 After an ugly lockout that cut the season in half, the Panthers started slowly in 1994-95. They never got any momentum with a three-game winning streak being the season high. In the end, they saw a playoff spot slip just out of reach in their second season just like they had in the first.

fourth overall) in that amateur draft or taking the fifth pick and going first in 1994. They chose the latter, and that meant they were "on the clock" from the close of the season until that first pick was announced.

While the Panthers needed offensive help, this was a draft deep with defensive talent.

While the Panthers needed offensive help, this was a draft deep with defensive talent. Unlike the

1993 draft, in which one defenseman was chosen in the first 10 picks, the 1994 draft saw three defensemen picked in the top 10, including the top two picks. The first pick, by the Panthers, was Ed Jovanovski of the Windsor Spitfires of the Ontario Hockey League. Jovanovski, a 6-2, 210 pounder, had some offensive skills, as evidenced by the fact that he was 10th among defensemen in the OHL in scoring with 51 points in 62 games. But his strength was his strength.

Bryan Murray, a successful former coach and general manager with Washington and Detroit, was hired August 1 as the new general manager. The decision was met with approval right away. He was hailed as a builder, a wheeler-dealer, a winner. He was billed as a coach who was willing to play young players, and he no doubt would push for the Panthers storehouse of youth to get the experience they needed.

"They have to play," he said. "If young players are good enough to play, I want the coach to give them ice time."

Torrey, who had taken over as the general manager with the departure of Clarke, was glad to get back to his other duties. And he was pleased that he was able to land someone with the capabilities of Murray. "Everywhere Bryan's gone in the business, he has done an outstanding job," Torrey said. "He's a good developer of young players.

"It's a crucial time for this franchise. The next year, the next two years, the decisions we're going to make on personnel are going to form the foundation of this franchise. Wayne and I decided that two heads are better than one."

The one he got on Murray's shoulders was a darned good one. He became the head coach of the Washington Capitals early in the 1981-82 season. Although the Caps did not make the playoffs that first year, Murray's .477 winning percentage was by far the best in team history. In fact, the 63 points the Caps earned under Murray were the third most in team history, even though he was not behind the bench for the first 14 games.

His second year with the team—1982-83—he led the Capitals to the playoffs for the first

"Ed is the guy who is going to be the horse of the defense for years to come," current general manager Bryan Murray said. "He is a dynamite hitter. He has a chance to be a star in this league."

"I love hitting guys," JovoCop said. "It's my forte. It's something that I grew up doing, and something that I'm going to keep on doing. I'm not the guy who is going to go out every night and score goals for our team, so I like to contribute in other ways, and playing physical is the way I like to contribute." Of course, for Jovanovski's star to rise, there had to be some stability in the franchise. One year and one general manager down, the next one coming in both cases. The Panthers had to get the right guy. Much progress had been made in the first year under Clarke, but could more progress be made?

The answer? An emphatic YES.

(Left) When Bryan Murray was introduced as the Panther's new general manager, he knew he inherited a team with a tight defense but one that had trouble scoring. (Above) While he had to find more offense, Jovanovski's talent was too much to pass up.

time ever. They did not miss again until the 1996-97 season. His specialty in Washington was defense. "With Bryan here, we were almost always able to keep the other team to three or fewer goals," said Kelly Miller, who played under Murray for four years in Washington. "Because of that, it gave our team a chance to win every single night. We were a hardworking team and I know from talking to players around the league, it was difficult to play the Capitals."

> **"Just hang in there, kid. You'll have a long career and win a lot of games."**

Murray was the NHL Coach of the Year in 1983-84 when the Capitals reached the 100-point mark for the first time in history. Their second-place finish was the first of five consec-

utive runner-up places under Murray. In 1988-89, he led the Caps to their only division title. In eight and a half seasons, he went 355-246-83 (a .580 winning percentage).

But after a slow start in the 1989-90 season, Murray was relieved of his duties. Ironically, it was another coach named Murray—his brother Terry—who replaced him.

Murray wasn't out of work long. The Detroit Red Wings snatched him up as coach and general manager for the 1990-91 season. Within two seasons, the Red Wings had won 15 more games than in the year before his arrival (one in which they didn't reach the playoffs) and finished in first place in the Norris Division. But that brought some wild expectations. "People were talking about winning the Cup in July," he said.

When the Red Wings were eliminated in the first round by Toronto in 1993, Murray was relieved of his coaching duties. Scotty Bowman was brought in to be the coach, and it was a combination that never meshed. Murray also was hurt—in his own estimation—by a trade he refused to make. The Red Wings needed a front-line goaltender; the prevailing thought was that Tim Cheveldae couldn't lead the team to the Stanley Cup. Murray had an option to trade two young players—winger Keith Primeau and goalie Chris Osgood—for Grant Fuhr, but he didn't do it. "I wouldn't do that," Murray said. "I thought it would hurt the franchise too much. That was a wrong deal, but if I did it, I might have kept that job."

Murray even contacted Clarke to see if the Panthers were willing to deal either Vanbiesbrouck or Fitzpatrick. Clarke wasn't willing, and Murray traded Cheveldae to Winnipeg for goalie Bob Essensa. Essensa wasn't the answer as the Red Wings lost to the third-year San Jose Sharks in the first round. Red Wings owner Mike Ilitch was ready to clean house and Murray was the first to go. Once again, the wait for another job would be short. Torrey, who remembered Murray from his early Capitals days, called. Murray listened.

"I remember my first game on Long Island," he recalled. "The Islanders squeaked out a victory over us. Bill came over to me and said, 'Just hang in there, kid. You'll have a long career and win a lot of games.'"

Murray did that. He accumulated 467 wins (sixth most in NHL history) to go with 337 losses and 112 ties for a winning percentage of .571 (eighth highest all-time for coaches with at least 600 games).

With that kind of resume, it is somewhat puzzling why he would accept a role with a new franchise. It was "common knowledge" that new

teams could not be competitive for several years. Someone with so much experience with winning would have difficulty accepting losing.

The fact is, he wouldn't have to. "We're not only interested in making the playoffs, we're also interested in being recognized as one of the good teams, and fairly soon," he said. "People are going to be paying more attention to the Panthers this year than they may have done last year. A lot of the same players will be in place. But some time down the road a little more skilled players in a couple of spots will have to be added."

Looking back more than two years later, he recalled his feelings for the franchise when he

arrived. "I didn't pay a lot of attention to Florida when I was in Detroit," he said. "They were in the other conference. But very definitely they were hard to play against. With Roger Neilson, they played a neutral-zone trap and basically a defense-first philosophy. They stayed in every game. If you beat them, you

(Left) The Panthers didn't have to change their aggressive style to fit Murray's style. And while he may have lost his job in Detroit because he wouldn't pull the trigger on a trade, he proved he was willing to deal with the acquisitions of players like Sheppard (above).

beat them 3-2 or 2-1, unless you were an exceptionally good team. There weren't that many teams dominating Florida."

Lockout Looms!

Murray hit the ground running. His fondness of young prospects, which may have cost him the Detroit job, would be tested with the young Panthers. His first job was to get Jovanovski signed. He also had to assess the talent he had and where the improvements were needed. If this team was going to be his team, he had work to do.

Unfortunately, shortly after he took over, there wasn't much work that could be done. At an impasse with the National Hockey League Players' Association, the owners were setting the stage for a lockout as training camps opened in early September. "LOCKOUT LOOMS" screamed the Toronto Sun, while newspapers across North America had similar sentiments.

It had been a year since the previous labor agreement had expired, and the owners were not willing to go another year without a new one. As with baseball, the main disagreement revolved around the owners wanting to institute a league-wide salary cap, while the players wanted nothing of the sort. There also was some dispute about the idea of a "franchise player" for each team. The owners wanted to protect one player from free agency, while the players nixed the idea. Also, the owners offered a more lenient free agency system for the rest of the players in exchange for the elimination of salary arbitration.

But the salary cap was the hub of the discussion, and the other issues were spokes that connected to it. At the last minute, the owners reportedly lifted the demand of a cap in exchange for a rookie cap, but the players wouldn't bite.

"We have said from the outset it needn't be a salary cap," Bettman said. "We could invent the generation system, and we have indicated a willingness to do that." But the players viewed tying salaries to revenues as a veiled attempt at a cap.

As September 4 and the opening of training camps approached, there was speculation that the lockout would cancel training camps. However, that played into the hands of the players. The players would not start earning regular paychecks until the regular season started. Meanwhile, the owners would lose money because of gate revenues for exhibition games. They also would have to cancel exhibition games in Europe (Winnipeg did play two games in Finland), where the league was hoping to make a major splash.

The owners decided to open training camps, but the problem was far from solved. While the sides met during training camp, no progress was made. With four days left before the regular season was scheduled to begin, the owners submitted another proposal, which was soundly rejected by the players. "The proposal they have is unacceptable," NHLPA executive director Bob Goodenow said. "In essence, it caps salaries and that is a big problem for us."

Bettman sounded equally discouraged by the lack of progress. "I wish we could say that we made a lot of progress but that hasn't been the case," he told reporters.

With little hope of a last-minute settlement, the possibility of a delay at the start of the season seemed likely. Unlike the threats of cancellation that surrounded training camp but never materialized, Bettman said emphatically that the regular season would not start without a new agreement.

After the latest proposals were rejected, there seemed little hope that the lockout could be avoided. And while Murray thought it might end quickly, many believed it would last a while, too. "I saw it coming for the past two or three years because players are making enough money to sustain without working," said Phil Esposito, the general manager of the Tampa Bay Lightning and an 18-year NHL veteran. "In my day, we couldn't."

when, on October 1, the lockout of players officially began.

Instead of lacing on the skates and going out and passing and shooting a round, hard-rubber puck, the players had time on their hands. Instead of formulating a game plan and breaking down game film, the coaches had time on their hands. Instead of orchestrating trades and scouting other team's players, the scouts and front-office personnel

The final clue that the season would be postponed came when the league canceled the waiver draft. League rules require the draft be held within seven days of the start of the season. With the start perilously hanging by a thread, seven days from what? All the doomsayers finally were right

had time on their hands.

"I keep hoping some player is going to drop in just to talk about something," Neilson said after only three days of the lockout. "It's a little weird." And while Neilson was optimistic

● *With the lockout official, players like Niedermayer (above) had plenty of time for deep contemplation. When would they get to play again? Would a work-stoppage ruin the progress of the previous year? Would the new fans put up with the interruption?*

that the lockout would be short-lived, Vanbiesbrouck, the Panthers' player representative, wasn't so sure.

"There has to be moderation in everything."

"There's a lot to be done," he said. "Once you put out one fire, you can get to the next. But it's going to take some time to get through all there is to resolve."

In the meantime, hobbies got renewed attention. Unlike many teams in the NHL, the Panthers saw a lot of their players stay in the area. "We had picnics on the beach," Neilson said. "We had guys tubing in the ocean. It was an experience you would never get again in professional sports."

Unfortunately, work stoppages were something that were becoming commonplace in professional sports. While the two sides exchanged proposals throughout the fall, the trenches they were camped in were becoming deeper and deeper. "They really think we're going to fold our tent," New York Islanders player rep Troy Loney said. "It isn't in the cards. I don't think (Bettman) understands the hockey mentality."

"It was tough on me, because I like to get along," Vanbiesbrouck said when asked to look back on the situation two years later. "I like for everybody to be at harmony. I think that we have a dressing room full of those people. It became difficult because it was an all-out, gloves off war.

"It was a difficult time and one that you never want to go through again, but I really felt good about the camaraderie that developed between players. I don't think anybody had ever tested that before, and it just shows that we were a real solid group. We were trying to make it a better game.

"People always think that professional ath-

letes are the most greedy people possible, but there are a lot of guys out there who play the game for two or three years. You've got to touch those people. There are people who

have played for 20 years, but it was in the past and they virtually have nothing left. You've got to touch those people."

While that argument had merit, so did the owners' stance. "You want to be fair in what you're doing, but there has to be moderation in everything," Huizenga said recently. "It's not what you want to happen, but it was necessary to do it, and the owners decided to go ahead and make that decision. I think that was the right thing to do. If we had to do it over again, we'd probably do it the same way, but if we had to do it over again, we'd try to figure out how not to have the problem to begin with."

For people like Greg Bouris, then the team's director of public and media relations, it was particularly tough. He was an employee of the team, yet he had established relationships with the players through extensive daily contact. "There was a lot of stress and strain," he said. "We didn't know how long it was going to go. You're talking about an organization that had 100 days to prepare, and played for another 180 days, so we hadn't even been around for a whole year to expose our product to the people. Now we were suffering a setback. So we really didn't know what to expect.

"You had to separate your feelings from the situation, and the players do the same thing, for the most part. You had to do what was the right thing given who your employer was or what your side was. The players had to toe the association line. Others had to toe the team line.

"We were restricted from having any contact with the players. I'm sure there may have been people who might have had personal relationships with the 'other side.' And it wasn't to the point where if a player was going to a hospital or something and he needed some pictures, that we'd say no. But we didn't go to the practice rink to shoot the bull. That's the only way it was going to work for both sides.

"If you were face-to-face every day, looking at each other, thinking, 'It's because of you that I'm in this situation,' you're better off not being near them. I think that's why when it was over, although there were still some pretty bitter feelings by some of the hard-liners, it all got ironed out to the good of the game. I think everybody realized, 'OK, that's behind us, we're all adults. We both agreed upon this new Collective Bargaining Agreement. Now let's move forward.'"

The down time also allowed the promotional side of the team to try some things that may not have been possible if there had been a season going on. "I think the fact that we were in a new market worked to our advantage. I don't think anybody wanted to come down hard and choose sides. It also allowed us to try to do

something for the fans. We had Roger Neilson and the assistant coaches go over the X's and O's of hockey in what we called, 'Chalk Talk.' That was available for the fans and the media. A lot of the newspapers sent up their copy editors and staff. It was a real good way to educate the people and the media down here about the nuances of the game.

"We also told them what Florida Panthers hockey was. Everybody had heard the term, 'the neutral-zone trap.' Even some hockey experts don't really know what the trap is. People would say, 'They used the trap last night.' Or, 'They didn't use the trap last night.' So we tried to explain that.

"We kept some kind of a bond going with the fans, although we weren't reaching the masses that you would if you were playing. It allowed people to kind of stay active and keep hockey on the minds of some people, and to help educate them in the process."

While the Panthers were trying to keep their fans interested and educated, the talks continued without progress. By mid November, the 84-game schedule had been reduced to 60 games. By late December, it became obvious that to have a season at all, the dispute would have to be solved soon. Bettman said 50 games was the minimum schedule he would authorize. On December 29, the league informed the Players' Association that the season would have to start on January 16, or there would be

Huizenga (left) and the other owners felt that they had to take a firm stance, but their decisions left Neilson (above) and his coaching counterparts with nothing to do.

Bryan Murray

Ten years ago, Bryan Murray spent what must have seemed like a year behind the bench during one grueling playoff game. Murray's Washington Capitals had led the New York Islanders, three games to one and owned home-ice advantage in the best-of-seven divisional semifinals. But the Islanders won the next two games to force a Game 7.

The teams were tied, 2-2, at the end of regulation, one overtime, two overtimes and three overtimes. Finally, at 8:47 of the fourth overtime, at nearly 2 a.m., Pat LaFontaine scored to give the Islanders the game and the series.

If that experience taught Murray anything, it taught him that he didn't like to wait for results, maybe because the results you get when you wait are not the results you want.

With that mentality, Murray took over the Panthers following the completion of their first year. The Panthers had missed the playoffs by one point, establishing a record in professional sports for a first-year club. Murray didn't change much the first year, instead choosing to survey the talent he had and assess everyone's abilities.

Following that season, however, he made several changes, including replacing the popular head coach, Roger Neilson. Murray believed that with Neilson's coaching style, the Panthers always would be competitive, but never would be championship caliber.

"Very definitely the Panthers were hard to play against," he said of observing the team from a distance in their first year. "With Roger Neilson, they played a neutral-zone trap and a defense-first philosophy. They stayed in every game. If you beat them, you beat them 3-2 or 2-1, unless you were an exceptionally good team. There weren't that many dominating teams at that time against Florida.

"The defense was the one area that I really felt couldn't compete on a regular basis in the NHL. They had some real good stay-at-home guys, but didn't have many points off the blue line at all. I thought that was a short-coming. It was a strength in one way, in that they could stay competitive every night, but it was a short-coming when you're trying to make the playoffs. You get close, but you can't really get it done."

So he added Robert Svehla, Jason Woolley and Terry Carkner, but didn't gut the team in the process.

"When I came here, people told me right away, 'You'll be good when you get a whole new team. Get rid of all the expansion guys who were leftover guys, and bring your own draft picks or trades.' That's not true, obviously. We try very hard to respect what the players have given here. There are some trades that could have been made, but we just felt that loyalty on our part is very important as well."

Chuck Fletcher, assistant general manager and son of former Toronto Maple Leafs' Chief Operating Officer Cliff Fletcher, says the trades that weren't made may be more important than the trades that were. "People judge the general manager by the trades he makes," he said. "I've always said that you have to judge a general manager by the trades he doesn't make. The media often doesn't know about that, but I've been around enough to see that we've turned down a lot of opportunities to move some key players. A lot of teams have wanted John Vanbiesbrouck and Brian Skrudland and Scott Mellanby.

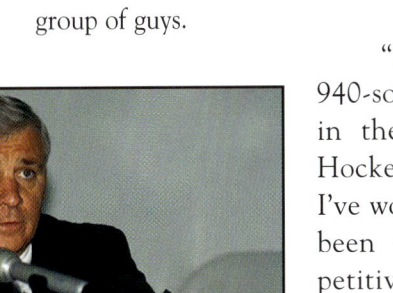

We've resisted a lot of tempting offers for draft picks and young players. We've done it because we want to build this consistency. We like the fact that the players know each other. We have a tremendous chemistry, and we're very hesitant to break that up.

"We picked up Svehla, who is an unbelievable defenseman. We signed Terry Carkner for nothing (in compensation). We got Jason Woolley. And these are key players on our team. We've gotten these players without really giving up very much. We haven't had to trade any of our veteran leadership at all."

Murray doesn't want to give up any edge he may have. He is fiercely competitive and doesn't want to lose, or tie. "Bryan wants to win, win every game," former Panthers director of public relations Greg Bouris said. "He's not looking at the mentality of wanting to tie every game and finish .500."

Murray agrees. "I'd like to think that I bring competitiveness as well as experience," he said. "I think I bring knowledge of talent. I think one of my strengths is that I can evaluate very well. I think I can look at players and decide whom to add to an already good group of guys.

"I coached 940-some games in the National Hockey League. I've won lots, I've been with competitive teams, teams that are very similar to the style we play here. I try to let people do their jobs. I hope I can share some ideas with them on occasion, whether it be about coaching or about player-personnel decisions. I think I bring respect to a staff of scouts and people off the ice as well. They like working here. They want to be here."

As do the players. "Guys want to be here, and why wouldn't they?," he said. "The environment in south Florida is awfully good. It's great to be able to get off the plane when you're coming from up north and be in 75° weather during the hockey season. We try to treat them right here. They've got a good coaching staff that communicates, and awfully good teammates that care about them."

And a general manager who is not willing to settle for anything but success.

 Murray had the option of clearing house when he arrived, but he chose to fine-tune instead. The results have been amazing, reaching the Stanley Cup Finals in his first year as head coach.

The agreement called for a 48-game schedule.

no season. That meant a deal would have to be struck by January 8 to allow ratification and a one-week training camp.

Things looked bleak.

But on January 11, three days past ground zero, the two sides reached an agreement, and the season was salvaged.

"After a while, we got to the point where it looked as if we were going to have to let a lot of people in the organization go, because we weren't bringing any revenue in," Bouris said. "Where the line would have been drawn, nobody knew. We got very, very close, probably within a few days of canceling the season.

"Fortunately enough, a new deal was struck, and work started, and everyone was happy to get back at it again. There were some bumps and bruises and some scars along the way, but in our situation it seems like it has been mended."

The agreement called for a 48-game schedule, with only intraconference games. Teams from the Eastern Conference would not play their counterparts from the West until the Stanley Cup Finals.

There would be no Anaheim vs. Florida. No rematch of the 1994 Stanley Cup Finals pitting the Rangers against Vancouver. No Montreal vs. Toronto.

But there would be a season.

"We were obviously very happy that the lockout was over," Huizenga recalled. "After having such a tremendous first season, we couldn't wait to get on to the second season. We needed to get back to the fans."

The season that left us short

The season was set to start January 21, as the Panthers traveled to Long Island to take on the team that claimed the last playoff spot in their place the previous year—the Islanders. Skrudland scored the first goal of the season, but Zigmund Palffy tied the score in the third period and then netted the game-winner 2:04 later to lift the Islanders to a 2-1 victory.

The Panthers also lost their next two games, including their home opener against Pittsburgh. In that game, the Panthers held a two-goal lead heading into the final period, but couldn't hold on. After the Pens had tied the score at 3-3, Stu Barnes scored to give the Panthers a 4-3 lead. But Joe Mullen scored on a power play with just over five minutes remaining and the game was tied again. Martin Straka

gave Pittsburgh the lead less than two minutes later and then Jaromir Jagr netted the insurance goal. Tom Fitzgerald brought Florida to within one goal at the 18:35 mark, but the Panthers could get no closer.

After a 3-2 loss at Tampa Bay—the Lightning's first victory over the Panthers—Florida stood 0-3-0. Was the first season a fluke? Did the work stoppage have a bigger effect on the young Panthers than on some more veteran teams? The answers resembled a turn indicator: yes, no, yes, no, yes, no.

On the heels of the three-game losing streak, the Panthers embarked on a three-game winning streak. The first win came in a return match with Tampa Bay. A road victory at Hartford was followed by an excep-

Once the season started, Vanbiesbrouck (left) and the Panthers had little room for error, but the result at the end of the 48-game schedule was hard for Nielson and his team to accept.

tional effort against Boston.

The Panthers traveled into Boston Garden and skated away with a 2-1 victory. Vanbiesbrouck was nearly flawless, stopping 38 of 39 Boston shots. With the win, the Panthers improved to 3-3-0, which slipped them into first place, the first time in team history they held that lofty perch alone.

Six games into the season, the Panthers already had achieved their season-best winning streak of three games (accomplished two more times), and were one game short of their longest losing streak of the year. It also marked the only time all season that they were at .500.

The Panthers went 1-2-1 over the next four, including a 7-3 debacle in Pittsburgh. But right after that game, the Beezer stopped all 26 of Philadelphia's shots in a 3-0 victory, the Panthers' first in Philadelphia. After two more wins in the next three games, the light went out again, and a four-game losing streak followed.

"We owned Patrick Roy. We chased him from the nets."

Wins over Ottawa bumpered both ends of the losing streak. Fitzpatrick shut out the Senators, 2-0, before the streak, then beat them again, 4-1, to end the streak. They hardly had momentum, though, as they prepared to travel to Madison Square Garden to face the defending champion Rangers. The Panthers never had earned a point in that building, and they hardly seemed like a team ready to explode.

They didn't. But then, neither did the Rangers. The two teams played to the only 0-0 tie in the league during the 1995 season. Vanbiesbrouck was named first star after stopping 44 shots. The Panthers managed only 23 shots. It was the first time the Panthers had been shut out all season. It wouldn't be the last.

During their first season of competition, the Panthers never lost by more than four goals. But when the New Jersey Devils scored five goals in 6:10 of the second period on March 3, that mark fell. The Devils won, 6-1, the first of three times that the Panthers would lose by five goals.

Of course, coming off that kind of loss, it was only natural to think the Panthers would mail it in the next couple of nights. Right. The Senators came to town and the Panthers handed them another setback, this time 3-2. That began the Panthers' second three-game winning streak of the season. A 2-0 shutout on the Panthers' last trip into historic Boston Garden, and a 4-1 victory at Hartford Civic Center left the Panthers with a 10-12-3 mark and in the middle of the playoff hunt with half a season remaining.

Then the turn indicator went off, again. Three losses in the next four games—all in overtime—killed the momentum. Tom Fitzgerald turned it back on for the next game, scoring two goals and adding an assist in a 3-2 win in Montreal. The Panthers won both times in Montreal in 1993-94 and stood 3-0-0 all-time in hallowed Montreal Forum. Counting their games in Florida, the Panthers stood 4-1-2 all-time against the most storied franchise in professional sports history.

"We pretty much dominated the Canadiens the first couple of years of our history," Bouris said. "We owned Patrick Roy. We chased him from the nets."

Figuring out the 1995 Panthers was next to impossible. Just when you thought they would be down, they were up, and vise versa. Coming off a big win in Montreal, the Panthers would be ready for Buffalo, right? A 3-0 Buffalo shutout. They would be down after that, right? They handed Pittsburgh its first shutout in two years. It was the Panthers' first victory ever against the Penguins.

A tie against Hartford and a victory at Tampa Bay set up a big game at home against the Rangers. Certainly the indicator would shine brightly on that night. Off. Mike Richter

the two teams had played, the Devils chased Fitzpatrick from the nets after their five-goal second-period barrage. Fitzpatrick was in the pipes again this night, but the Devils couldn't get the puck past him.

"It's certainly nice to look up (at the scoreboard) after the game and see a zero," Fitzpatrick said. "Last game I got blown out,

handed the Panthers their first home shutout in team history, 5-0. Following that whitewashing, the Panthers went 1-2-1 in their next four games, which left them in a crunch to make the playoffs.

The Devils came into Miami Arena on a hot streak. They had entered the game tied for fourth in the Eastern Conference and also owned a 5-0-2 record all-time against the Panthers. The last time

but it's nice to get a win. The good chances that they did have I saw the puck. It certainly makes my job easier when I don't have to stop screened shots or slap shots from the slot."

The Panthers stood tied with Tampa Bay for 11th in the conference following the game. Eight teams made the playoffs from each conference, so there still were hurdles

The Panthers had a big game at home against the Rangers, but New York's Mike Richter stopped Dave Lowry and kept the Cats out of the net. It started the Cats on a 1-3-1 skid.

to clear. Against Quebec in the next game, Robert Svehla scored his first NHL goal to help the Panthers to a three-goal first period in a 4-2 victory. The Panthers then traveled to Ottawa to face the Senators once again. The Panthers owned a 6-0-1 all-time record against the Senators, including 3-0-0 in Ottawa.

You can only slide so far until, like California, you're going to fall into the ocean."

The Senators scored first when Sylvain Turgeon got the puck past Vanbiesbrouck. Belanger tied the score a minute and a half later, and the teams went to the first intermission tied at 1-1. The rest of the game was all Panthers. Mellanby opened the scoring in the second period and Johan Garpenlov increased the lead to 3-1 at the end of the second. Garpenlov scored again in the third period and Jody Hull added an empty netter in the final minute.

The victory left the Panthers with 41 points, good for a tie for 10th with Montreal. The Rangers and the Whalers were two points ahead. Buffalo was a point better than the Rangers and Whalers, and Washington had one more than the Sabres. There were three spots to divvy up between the six teams.

"It's sort of like the playoffs for us," Neilson said. "It's the first round. We play every other night and we've got to win or we're out."

Neilson became the prophet he didn't want to be. The Panthers traveled to Buffalo, where Dominik Hasek blanked them for the second time in a month and two days, 5-0. The Sabres scored three goals in a span of 1:41 to blow open a close game. "He was the difference in the game again, the same as the last two games we played

against him," Mike Hough said. "He's been the difference the whole time. You've got to tip your hat to him. He played really well."

Not only did the Sabres win, thereby gain-

ing two points on the Panthers, but so did Washington and the Rangers. Montreal tied its game, pulling one point ahead of the Panthers in 10th place. With four games remaining, the

Panthers were four points out of the final play-off spot with two teams in between.

The Panthers then traveled to New Jersey and fell to the Devils, 3-1. That left them in dire measures with three games remaining. Still, their playoff hopes were _almost_ in their own hands. The Panthers closed the home portion of their schedule against the Capitals. A victory in that game and a Rangers loss at Philadelphia would put the Panthers in control of their own fate. They would need to win their last two, including one at the Rangers, and they would be in.

First things first.

They had to beat Washington. Skrudland wanted no part of "what-ifs."

"Hindsight is something you hate to look back on," he said. Right, Brian, and experience takes time. "I'd like to think we're capable of winning these next three games, but something in the back of my mind is telling me that may not be enough. We are still optimistic to a point, but you can only slide so far until, like California, you're going to fall into the ocean."

The big quake happened in the form of a 2-2 tie against the Caps and a 2-0 Rangers victory in Philly. The Panthers were polite in their game, which is another way to say they were not the least bit offensive. They managed one shot in the first period. Fortunately, Vanbiesbrouck didn't allow any goals and the first period ended score-less. Bob Kudelski scored

at 2:18 of the second period to give Florida a 1-0 lead. The Caps' Keith Jones scored the next two goals, and Belanger scored the final home goal for the Panthers to forge the final score.

"We gave it everything we had, but we just couldn't quite do it," Neilson said.

For the second straight season, the Panthers were eliminated with games left to play. In the first campaign, there was just one game to play, a home game against the Islanders. This time, road games at the Rangers and the Penguins were the meaningless contests. Like the year before, the Panthers won the games that didn't matter. Both games ended 4-3 and the Panthers once again finished one point out of the playoffs.

"I know the guys are sick and tired of this happening," Skrudland said. "This is only two years of it and I know how disappointed we are. I know we've got a lot of pride in this dressing room, to a man."

To a man, however, this Panthers team had represented South Florida extremely well in the first two years. A 53-56-23 mark after two years was nothing to sneeze at. One point out of the playoffs was reason for optimism. And in a sport where gate revenues are a huge portion of total revenues, the Panthers played to an average of 14,192 fans per game at home. That represents 97 percent of capacity.

Some resentment to the lockout, huh?

 Garpenlov (left), Paul Laus (above) and the Panthers battled the Capitals to a 2-2 tie, which kept them out of the playoffs. For the second straight year, they missed by one point.

In each of their first two seasons, the Florida Panthers finished near .500 and one point out of the playoffs. While that is a remarkable record for a team in its infancy, it was a troubling thought if it was to be a pattern. So as they headed into season No. 3, the higher-ups for Florida made a gutsy move. They fired Roger Neilson.

The same Roger Neilson who had guided them to a professional-sports best .494 winning percentage in their inaugural year. The same Roger Neilson who had taught the Panthers the neutral-zone trap that made them one of the better defensive teams in the league.

"I felt we needed a change in philosophy," new general manager Bryan Murray said. "The way we were going, we could be a team that could play in the middle of the pack and have a chance to make the playoffs every year, but not necessarily make them or do well in them. I didn't see any way we were going to get any better, because our young players weren't getting a chance to play. I felt very strongly that you can't play defense only in this league and become one of the better teams. I wanted to play Rob Niedermayer more. I wanted to make sure that Ed Jovanovski got in the lineup (once he was signed). I felt like that wouldn't happen with Roger.

"Secondly, I felt that we had adopted the philosophy of just being competitive. That may be good enough for some people, but not for me. I really felt that in a new market, we had to entertain our fans a little bit more with a style change. We've opened up the game as a result of it."

It is no surprise that Neilson does not agree. In fact, nearly two years later, he says he doesn't understand the decision. "We (Neilson and assistant coach Craig Ramsey who was fired with Neilson) thought we had done as good a job as we could," he said. "We thought the team had done very well.

"The whole idea was that we would go with veteran players and put our young players in when they were ready. After two years, many of the young players were starting to develop. I was very excited about the next year. We were 12-10-3 over the last 25 games in year two. We all felt the team was in a very good position."

Neilson's position is that the team was on the verge of major success and while Doug MacLean (his replacement) "made all the right moves," that the team would have been successful if he were still the coach. "I don't think it would have mattered who had been coaching last year. I'm sure the team would have improved."

One thing no one disputes is that Neilson's impact on the franchise was huge and positive. And those thoughts come from some unexpected sources. "There probably wasn't a better guy for me to come in and play for to learn the defensive side of the game," said Rob Niedermayer, the frustrated young player whose untried skills may have been the biggest reason for Neilson's departure. "That's one of the areas of my game that really needed work."

Huizenga, the owner of the team, said he "really liked Roger and wanted to do right by him."

How about these glowing comments? "The reason the Panthers finished one point out of the playoffs in their first year was good coaching. I think Roger came in and gave confidence to a lot of players.

Over the hump

The Panthers came out of the chute bearing their teeth after missing the playoffs in each of their first two years in the league, nailing down the fourth seed in the Eastern Conference playoffs.

Remember that expansion brought us left-over guys who were not among the top 15 guys on their former teams.

"Roger played a defensive system in his whole career that was as good as any that any other coach ever had in this league. Guys knew how to play. They were educated how to play. He is a very patient person, and a guy you can respect. He is a great guy, and a hard-working guy whose life was coaching.

"You ask any player who ever played for Roger about him, and 99 percent of them would tell you he is a heck of a man and a heck of a coach. There was no question he did a real fine job here."

Those words came from Murray, the man who fired him.

"There is no sane way to justify it, no adequate rationale to explain away the blood on the ice."

But each of those comments had an addendum. Murray says, "His philosophy just happened to be different from mine." Niedermayer recalls that after his first couple of seasons, "I was kind of wondering if I could play in this league. I wasn't contributing as much as I would have liked. My confidence was way down."

Huizenga listened to Murray and Torrey, who explained the change in philosophy as the reason that the move was necessary. "Bill came in and said, 'Wayne, you know this won't be popular, and I know it may not seem like the right thing to do, but we've got to move forward.' I took the usual chicken way out and told him if that's what he thought we should do, then go ahead and do it."

Former director of public and media relations Greg Bouris, who had the unenviable

task of explaining the change to the puzzled media, cites the difference in the terms of the goals of general managers and coaches. "They have the same common goal and that's to win," he said. "But they have very different day-to-day goals. The coach has to win today, or else he may not be here tomorrow. The general manager wants to win today, but he has to plan for the future."

The media didn't buy it.

"Neilson on ice: That's cold" screamed *The Miami Herald* headline. Underneath that banner, Greg Cote wrote, "There is no sane way to justify it, no adequate rationale to explain away the blood on the ice. Roger Neilson was fired for no good reason. Ruthlessly, suddenly and without class, the Panthers indulged the power play of General Manager Bryan Murray. It is, in every sense of the word, a shame. It is unseemly. It stinks."

Later in the same article, Cote wrote, "Absent any reason whatsoever to fire Neilson for what he accomplished, or didn't, the inventive Murray decided to make a preemptive strike. So he fired Neilson in anticipation of what he might not accomplish in the future. Insane."

Cote was not alone. David Neal, also of *The Herald*, and Ray Murray, of the *Sun-Sentinel*, focused their stories on the reaction of the likable coach. Dave Joseph of the *Sun-Sentinel* predicted doom and gloom for the foreseeable future for the Panthers.

Of course, that didn't happen. Murray doesn't gloat now about the brilliance of the move. He gives the credit, instead, to MacLean, the coach he brought in to replace Neilson. Painted as a power-hungry egomaniac by the media, Murray thought

only about the team's future. And though he knew that the move would be tough for fans and media to accept, he felt strongly enough about the decision that he stuck by it. "In expansion, like in any business, there is a certain point where you have to make some hard decisions," he said. "If you're a businessman, you have to know when to break the ties with the guy who helped you establish the business but doesn't want it to get bigger. I wanted this team to change from a defense-only team to a team that could, in the very near future, compete with the elite teams in the league. I wanted a team that would allow the young players not only to develop, but become important. This has been my philosophy all the way through.

"I felt that if we stayed with Roger, we would set that timetable back a little bit. It was an extremely difficult decision, but I felt that we had to do something."

If Murray needed something to take his mind off the firing, and the reaction to it, he only had to wait one day. Ed Jovanovski, the first-round pick in 1995, had not been signed the previous year and had spent the season playing for Windsor of the Ontario Hockey League. On the day after Neilson was jettisoned, Jovanovski came aboard.

"Ed may be as good a raw talent as there is in the league," MacLean said. "He has a chance to be a superstar."

One player who already was a superstar was John Vanbiesbrouck. He headed the list of three Panthers free agents during the 1995 off-season. Vanbiesbrouck was an unusual free agent, due to a clause in the transition rules to

The fact that young players like Niedermayer (#44, left) felt like Neilson always was looking over their shoulder may have been the downfall of the otherwise popular coach.

the new collective bargaining agreement. In fact, he, Steve Thomas of the Islanders and Ulf Samuelsson of the Penguins were the only three players in the league who fell into this special category.

Under these transition rules, any free agent who was exactly 31 years old on

> **"What I don't like about free-agency is that you don't grow up with the team."**

June 30, 1995, required a qualifying offer equal to 115 percent of the player's previous year's salary in order for the club to retain a right of first refusal for the player. Unlike those of other restricted free agents, Vanbiesbrouck's, Thomas' and Samuelsson's teams would not be entitled to compensation (up to five first-round picks) as the Panthers thought they would. It made it more imperative to sign the star goalie.

The business of free agency was a big issue in the labor dispute. The players wanted a more lenient system and the owners wanted to restrict it with a salary cap. Huizenga, one of the "hard-liners" according to the media, is not opposed to free agency because of the money. His objection is that of a fan.

"What I don't like about free agency is that you don't grow up with the team," he said. "In the old days, players played for one team. They were there for 20 years. You

tants, and if I want to keep the people who work for me, I've got to treat them right. I've got to pay them what the market demands, and they've got to do their job. So, free agency is not a problem to me.

"As long as we're going to have free agency, let everybody have one-year contracts. At the end of every year, let them do what's best for them, and we'll do what's best for us. That's what life is all about. I'm not against free agency.

don't find that today. That's the part I don't like about it. I'm not against free agency. I wouldn't care if every member of our team had a one-year contract. That wouldn't bother me at all.

"In my business, nobody has contracts. If I want to keep my assis-

"What bothers me is that the fans don't get a chance to see a guy like Jovanovski come in and stay with a team for a long period of time (without several contract disputes)."

Vanbiesbrouck (left) had been a cornerstone of the Panthers during their first two years, but with his free-agency and the dismissal of Neilson, he wondered where he would tend net nest. He turned out to be a key contributor to the Panthers' 1995-96 playoff run.

Vanbiesbrouck, even though he was the one bonafide star on the team, was not above the squabbles that go with contract negotiations. Whether it was posturing or not, Vanbiesbrouck used the firing of Neilson to vent some frustration. "They're obviously changing their direction," he said the day after Neilson's dismissal. "Who knows who they're going to include in that direction, but I think it's significant that I'm going to arbitration at the same time. I don't know how to put 2 and 2 together because nobody can predict the future." And though he had stated a few months earlier that he wanted to retire as a Panther, he changed that response, too.

"A lot of the older players were wondering what would happen."

The Panthers were undaunted by the talk and extended a qualifying offer to the Beezer, maintaining the team's rights to him. With the right to match any offer he received, the Panthers were certain they could keep Vanbiesbrouck if they wanted to. Now the mending had to take place.

The Panthers also had to prepare for the amateur draft, one in which they had the 10th pick overall. After choosing fifth and first the previous two years, the Panthers' choices were not so obvious. They selected Radek Dvorak, a 6-2, 185-pound right winger from the Czech Republic. Dvorak was converted to left wing by the Panthers, and he had the big-play potential that the Panthers needed. "Radek is a great skater, with great hands and great hockey instincts," Murray said. "He has a chance to be a top player in the NHL."

The Panthers chose four wingers, three defensemen and two goalies in the 1995 draft.

The next step was to name the man who would lead them into the next season. When Neilson was fired, the *Sun-Sentinel* listed six choices as possible candidates. Some had previous NHL head coaching experience, others were current minor league coaches. MacLean was not on the list. In fact, while Murray may have thought about the possibility briefly, MacLean was not at the top of his initial list either.

"It took a long time to find the right guy," he said. "It was a very hard time. Finding the right guy was a process." Eventually, that process led Murray to MacLean. MacLean had been Murray's assistant coach in Detroit for the 1990-91 season. The next season, he was promoted to associate coach, and the following year he was named assistant general manager. He served in that role for two years, until Murray was fired. When Murray was hired to replace Bob Clarke, MacLean left the Red Wings to become the director of player development and head scout of the Panthers.

On July 24, 1995, MacLean was introduced as the new coach of the Panthers. "I knew Doug," Murray said, "but I wanted to go through a number of other candidates. I guess it was probably instinctive as much as anything else. That, and knowledge about the individual. I didn't have nearly as much about the other candidates as I did Doug.

"I just felt that he could communicate. He also had a philosophy somewhat similar to mine. Most importantly, he was very interested in playing young players and developing a program. We're both in this for the long term, not the short term."

MacLean knew he was heading into a boiling pot. Every step would be scrutinized. Unless he achieved a record at least as good as Neilson did, the switch would be further chastised. He didn't care.

"I guess I was so excited to get an opportunity that I didn't really spend a lot of time worrying about comparing myself to Roger," he said. "There was some pressure because Roger was a popular guy, a good coach and did a real good job. But I knew that this was the opportunity of a lifetime and I had to make the best of it, and I

didn't spend a lot of time thinking about that."

What he did spend his time doing was preparing the team his way. "I had lots of support, Lindy Ruff, Duane Sutter, Billy Smith, Bryan Murray, Bill Torrey, Chuck Fletcher, an unbelievable management team. And let's not kid ourselves, if it wasn't for the help I got from them as a group, it would have been a lot tougher. You go from there to the Skrudlands and the Vanbiesbroucks and people like that that I got support from; it certainly made it easier."

Skrudland recalls the period after MacLean's appointment. "A lot of the older players were wondering what would happen," he said. "Was he going to

Dvorak's (left) big-play ability made him a good choice as the Panthers' No. 1 pick in the amateur draft. MacLean (above) brought intensity to the Panthers' bench, but he also was willing to listen to the counsel of his older players, who told him he had talent on his team.

come in and start shuffling everybody in and out? Doug came to me right off the bat, and I said to him, 'We've got a very committed group here. I think you'll notice that from day one when you come in. Each and every guy comes to play. We all want to win. We'd go the extra mile to win. I think you've got a good group also to teach some of our good young players.'

"Doug's reaction was, 'As long as we're going to win, as long as guys are going to commit, we're not going to make wholesale changes. I've seen you guys play as well.'"

MacLean got a chance to see his younger players for the first time as the head coach when the Panthers hosted a five-day condi-

"For the amount of money we spend on...evaluating talent, we don't do enough developing that talent,"

tioning camp for the top 25 prospects in the organization. With the big reason MacLean replaced Neilson being willingness to play the younger players before they could be key contributors, MacLean had to know how these guys played. All the Panthers draft picks in their first three amateur drafts attended, with the exception of Dvorak and Rhett Warrener. Dvorak stayed in the Czech Republic, where young players play virtually year-round. Warrener already was enrolled in a skating-acceleration program.

"For the amount of money we spend on recognizing and evaluating talent, we don't do enough developing that talent," assistant general manager Chuck Fletcher said before the camp started. "Now that we have built up 25 prospects, we hope to do this every summer."

MacLean found aggressive talent that fit his and Murray's style. "Sometimes your coaching style is dictated by what you have to work with," the new coach said. "And in fairness to the people who were before me, Bryan had made a lot of changes in personnel. He added six new defensemen from when Roger was here and five or six forwards.

"We already had an aggressive group of people: Billy Lindsay, Tommy Fitzgerald, Bryan Skrudland and these types, the (Dave) Lowrys and (Scott) Mellanbys, they're aggressive-type players. When we added a little more offense from the blue line, a little more aggressiveness on the blue line, a little more speed on the blue line— with the emergence of Niedermayer and Dvorak and all these people—it allowed us to play a more aggressive game."

Dvorak was added officially to the fold on August 8, with the expectation he could contribute right away. "Radek is a world-class player," Murray said at his signing. "He has a chance to make this team." Dvorak had caught the attention of the Panthers in the World Under-17 Tournament in 1993. He was a member of the Czech team that reached the semifinals.

"Radek was the best player in the tournament, by a fairly wide margin," said Paul Henry, the scout who scouted him in the tournament. "I became absolutely overwhelmed by him." Henry thought the only reason Dvorak lasted until the 10th pick overall was a broken hand he suffered the previous season.

The month following Dvorak's signing, the Panthers inked another key figure. Duane Sutter, one of six brothers to play in the NHL, was added to the coaching staff to replace Craig Ramsey. Though he no longer wore the skates during the game, Sutter's presence on the ice in practice has helped the team's progress.

"Duane is a competitive, hard-nosed guy," Murray said. "Every game is a critical game for him. He played hard and tough and I think he can communicate that to our players. The players know his background. They respect it.

"I know the way we operated in the past. You could almost tell guys what to do and they had no choice but to do it. Today, the collective bargaining agreement

doesn't allow you to send players to the minors nearly as easily, so you've got to communicate. You've got to get the best out of them. When you bring a player aboard, he's got to respect and comply with the rules, but you've got to be fair

Skrudland (left) and Dvorak (above) represent opposite ends of the spectrum for the Panthers. Skrudland, the wily veteran, was called on to mentor the rookies like Dvorak.

Doug MacLean

Doug MacLean took over a third-year franchise with huge expectations. Everyone expected him to be a big failure.

MacLean was a virtual unknown. He had been an assistant coach in the NHL, but never was the main man behind the bench. His predecessor, Roger Neilson, was a veteran of nearly 30 years in the coaching ranks. He had coached six teams prior to his stint with the Panthers, and he had been successful nearly everywhere. He had led the Panthers to the best record in professional sports history for a club in its first year in an existing league and conference.

Neilson was a known commodity and the future appeared to be bullish with him at the helm. Instead, he was let go, and MacLean stepped in.

Failure? What failure? MacLean has spent exactly one game with a career (or single-season) losing record. The Panthers lost his first game against the defending Stanley Cup champion New Jersey Devils, then embarked on a four-game winning streak. They finished his first season 41-31-10. In his second year, he led the team to an 8-0-4 mark out of the gate. How did he do it? He instilled confidence in everybody around him.

"He's the sort of guy who even after tough losses will sit down with the players and have a little fun as well as get a point across," general manager Bryan Murray said. "He doesn't try to be the star of the show. He is open-minded. He's got an open-door policy that is really important with today's athletes. He communicates and he's a real honest guy. He's got excellent teaching skills."

"Doug has given a lot of the young guys confidence," Dave Lowry said. "He's played them in key situations. He's given them opportunities after mistakes. You look at a guy like Robby Niedermayer. He's taken the ball and he's run with it. He's now one of the key players on this hockey club. He's one of the go-to-guys. A couple of years ago Robby was struggling to find himself, and now he's a player full of confidence."

Niedermayer agrees. "He came in and kind of restored my confidence," he said. "For the first couple of years, I was wondering if I could play in this league. Since I wasn't contributing as much as I would have liked to, my confidence was way down. He came in and said right from the start, 'You're going to get a good chance to play, and if you make a mistake, we'll put you right back out there.' That's something that I really needed. It's really helped me."

Niedermayer is not the only player MacLean's style has helped. Ed Jovanovski, Radek Dvorak, Paul Laus, Robert Svehla and Rhett Warrener all played key roles in the Panthers run to the Cup finals, and they blossomed under MacLean.

"Doug is a players' coach, and he's got a players' staff," Murray said. "I think that's really important today. The way we operated in the past—in my first years in the league—you could almost tell guys what to do and they had no choice but to do it. Today the collective bargaining agreement doesn't allow you to send players to the minors nearly as easily, so you've got to communicate. You've got to get the best out of them. When you bring a player aboard, he's got to respect and comply with the rules, but you've got to be fair about them. I think our staff really allows that to happen. I think our players understand that, and obviously they work hard because of it."

Working hard has been part of MacLean's story his whole life. His father once told a story about Doug as a young student. He had his sights set on getting a 92 in a mathematics class. He brought home a 90 and was disappointed. Not too far from the situation last spring. The Panthers were not expected to travel far in the playoffs. A 90 (an A-) would be winning a couple of rounds, maybe even taking the Penguins to Game 7. Nobody would have blinked if the Panthers had lost that game on the road. But MacLean was not satisfied. He wanted that 92. Actually he wanted the 100— the Stanley Cup championship. But the 92 was within reach at that point, and he went after it with everything he had.

"There was no reason for them to play the way they did," said Denis Potvin, the team's television analyst. "They could have bowed out and no one would have said anything. It had a lot to do with the coach's character. You take his attitude about not being satisfied and combine it with his character, and it's obviously a good virus to go through the team."

While MacLean is not satisfied with anything but maximum performance, his looseness with his players may be one of his most important attributes. Once, during the 1995-96 season, Stu Barnes cheated in a little too far on offense, thus exposing the defense to a risky situation. MacLean chastised him, sort of.

"I hate it when you cheat like that," the coach said, "but I do love it when you score." When Barnes asked if he should take the same gamble again, MacLean responded, "If you're going to do that, you'd better score."

MacLean knew the offense had to be picked up if the team was going to proceed from mediocre to good. Just as Torrey had said that a team can't win if it gives up 40 to 50 shots a night, a team can't win big if it only scores 2.77 and 2.40 goals per game, as the Panthers did in their first two seasons, respectively.

"Doug has opened it up," Lowry said. "He inherited a hockey club that was very sound defensively. When a coach has confidence that a team can play strong defensively, and he opens it up, he allows them to take chances. He knows that if the chance doesn't work out, guys are going to get back. Doug knows our guys know how to play in their own end of the ice."

The fact that MacLean took the time to know his players, as people as well as their hockey skills, impressed those players. "When Doug took over, a lot of the older players at the time were wondering just exactly what would happen, how we were all going to make out," captain Brian Skrudland said. "Were they going to come in and just start shuffling everybody in and out? I said to him, 'We've got a very committed group here. I think you'll notice that from day one when you come in. Each and every guy comes to play. We all want to win. We'd go the extra mile to win. I think you've got a good group to also teach some of our good young players.'

"His response was very straightforward. He said, 'As long as we're going to win, as long as guys are going to commit, don't worry, I'm not coming in here to make wholesale changes. I've seen you guys play as well.'

"Things have been pretty positive since."

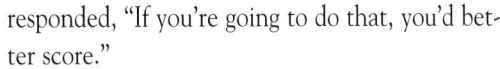

MacLean is a perfectionist, yet he also is a players' coach. His use of young players instilled confidence in those players that proved vital to the team's success during the run to the Finals.

about them. I think our staff really allows that to happen. I think our players understand that, and obviously they work hard because of it."

With training camp ready to open, there was a lot of uncertainty and excitement surrounding the team. Would MacLean be able to mix the young talent with the veterans? Would the team be able to get over the hump and make the playoffs? Where would the team play after this season? That bomb was dropped just before training camp.

With the team losing approximately $1 million per month in the Miami Arena, Huizenga was busy looking for other options. After failing to find a municipality willing to build an arena, Huizenga set the wheels in motion to leave South Florida. Dean Jordan, the team's executive vice president, sent a letter to the Miami Sports and Exhibition Authority stating that the team would not renew its lease for the 1996-97 season under the current lease conditions.

"Vanbiesbrouck said I got a 'rat trick.'"

Huizenga was hopeful of staying in the area, and he still was talking to officials in all three metro counties. But he also acknowledged that he would consider selling the team to investors from other cities. Officials from Nashville, Tennessee, had a standing offer to any NHL or NBA team owner to get them to move. The offer included a $20 million relocation fee, nearly all of the ticket revenue, 97.5 percent of skybox revenue, all advertising revenue and more than half the parking revenue.

Huizenga maintained his primary interest was to stay in the area. "There are plenty of cities that would like to have a National Hockey League franchise," he said. "But that is not what we are trying to do. We are trying to find a way to keep it here."

Huizenga promised to spend a "substantial" sum of money to help secure a local arena, and he wouldn't require ownership of the arena. But the difference would have to be made up with public money, and there was not much sign that any municipality or county would be willing to foot the bill entirely on its own.

Finally, training camp arrived and an off-season of turmoil and uncertainty gave way to the crack of sticks on the ice, the ping of pucks hitting the post and the shouts of coaches' instruction to the players. The uncertainty still remained, especially regarding where the team would call home in the future, but at least there was action to talk about.

The Panthers won their first preseason game and lost the second, but a key in both games was the play of Niedermayer. Niedermayer had suffered from a lack of confidence under Neilson and had seldom played to his potential. When Murray brought in MacLean, one of the first things the new coach did was tell the young center that he would be an important part of the team, and that he would get his ice time no matter what. After two preseason games, MacLean had seen enough of the new Niedermayer and designated him the assistant captain.

"I want him to be a main man for us this year," MacLean said at the time. Niedermayer responded, "This is a huge year for me. It's time for me to start contributing. My first two years were kind of frustrating. I didn't play as well as I should have."

The regular season opened with the Panthers on the road in New Jersey facing the defending Stanley Cup champions. The Devils must like the numeric progression 4-0. That was the result in games in the Finals against Detroit the previous spring, and that was the score against the Panthers to open defense of their Cup. It would be the last time all season that the Panthers were below .500.

The Cats returned to Miami Arena for Game 2 of the season where they entertained Calgary. The final score was 4-3 in favor of Florida. Jesse Belanger and Jody Hull each scored and Mellanby scored three, which, of course, makes five. It just happens that one of Mellanby's wasn't on the ice.

Let Mellanby tell it. "We were just getting ready to go out onto the ice for the start of the game, and somebody yelled that there was a rat running down the hall," he said. "It came right into our locker room. It just started scurrying around and it then came right at me. I hit it like a slap shot, threw it about 10 feet across the room, where it hit the wall and it was dead.

"In the game, I had a couple of goals. When the press came in, John Vanbiesbrouck said I got a 'rat trick.'"

Mellanby's "rat trick" prompted the appearance of packs of rats during the 1995-96 season, in the form of dressed-up humans (above) and a plastic deluge (following pages).

Word got out to the public. When Mellanby netted a goal a couple of games later, a few fans threw plastic rats onto the ice. After a while, any time a Panther scored, the fans threw rats.

"It just snowballed," Mellanby said. "At first and for awhile, I wasn't sure how I felt about it. I kind of felt a little bit embarrassed by it. I kind of felt like I was responsible for this. But as it went along, I came to appreciate it a little more. In the playoffs, it was phenomenal.

"I think it was great. It was part of our story. And it's something that I'm not even that disappointed is not there this year (1996-97), because I think it was unique to last season, and the way things just kind of evolved. Hopefully this year we won't have to kill a rodent or anything, but this season will develop its own identity. I think it's kind of a neat piece of the story."

They hired Orkin, the pest-control company, to clear the ice after each shower of rats.

And then, as an afterthought, he added, "Believe me, it was self defense. If it was a bigger animal, I probably would have been hiding behind somebody. Probably behind Paul Laus."

The Panthers took full advantage of the situation. They hired Orkin, the pest-control company, to clear the ice after each shower of rats. And while the NHL urged the team to try to control the fans, Huizenga's wife, Marti, led the barrage, and even wore different rhinestone-studded "rat" pins. The public address announcer was required to inform the fans that anyone caught throwing rats on the ice would be removed from the arena, but nobody really believed that Marti Huizenga would be escorted out.

"The rats pulled everything together," Wayne Huizenga said. "Everywhere you went, people were hanging rats from their mirrors in their cars. If the rat had a long tail, the driver would wrap it around the mirror. You'd be driving down the road and there might be a rat hanging in the back window. It was unbelievable."

Following another victory, 6-1 over Montreal, the Panthers got good news and bad news. The good news? Vanbiesbrouck agreed to a three-year $6.5 million deal, meaning he would be playing his home games in Miami for another three years. Maybe. That's the bad news. Huizenga met with Micky Arison, owner of the Heat, to discuss the possibility of building a waterfront arena to house both teams. The meeting, which culminated months of negotiations, broke up with Arison planning to go ahead on his own, and Huizenga steaming closer to his deadline to sell or move the team.

"I will not own a team that plays in downtown Miami," he said through a spokesman. Since Broward County already had put its best offer on the table—one that was rejected by Huizenga—Dade County apparently was the only option. And it didn't appear to be a good one.

Metro-Dade Commission Chairman Art Teele categorized their commission's efforts thusly: "We're just trying to keep from buying the caskets."

While the politicians were playing footsies, the Panthers were playing darned good hockey. Two more victories, and four in their next five games, left the Cats 6-2-0, the best record in the entire league.

"Early on, the way we started you had to say, 'This is our year. We're going to make the playoffs this year. There is no doubt about it,'" Huizenga said. And while the players were not talking about it publicly, they were talking about confidence in their new style of play. "Our system in the past was a more defensive style, which put pressure on the defensemen and goaltenders," defenseman Gord Murphy said. "We weren't able

to get big leads. Now, with the offense capable of scoring four or five goals every game, it definitely makes our job a little bit easier."

The Panthers finished October with a 7-4-0 record, with no two-game losing streaks, all the while fighting through several injuries. Jovanovski had not yet made his debut because of a broken finger, and Dave Lowry (four to six weeks with a knee sprain) and Jody Hull (a week with a cracked rib) went down on the same night.

But each time the Panthers lost a player, somebody else picked up the slack. Their fortune even seemed to transcend to the arena deal. Just when it appeared the team would be forced to leave town, the hotel and motel owners agreed to an increase in the bed tax that would help fund the arena in Broward County. There

still were many hurdles to clear, but at least there were discussions.

All the discussions in the NHL centered around the Panthers. On November 2, Jovanovski made his NHL debut in Philadelphia, Dvorak scored his first NHL goal and Vanbiesbrouck turned back 21 Flyers shots in a 2-1 victory. The Panthers followed that with six more victories in a row, a franchise record.

Dvorak was a scoring machine during the stretch. The night after the victory in Philly, he netted another goal. He followed that with two goals in consecutive games, giving him six in four games. Once his streak was stopped,

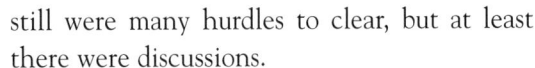
The Panthers' success was a total team effort. Rookies and veterans alike took roles of leadership throughout the season. Unlike many teams that counted on one or two lines, the Panthers had four lines that contributed, meaning opponents never had a chance to rest.

Vanbiesbrouck and Billy Lindsay took hold of the reins. The Beezer won six of the games in the streak, giving up just eight goals. Lindsay scored two goals and added an assist in win No. 6, a 4-1 victory over Buffalo.

In victory No. 7, Niedermayer, Robert Svehla and Stu Barnes keyed a third-period barrage that lifted Florida to a 5-2 decision over Toronto. "It's always different guys every night," Niedermayer said after the game. "It's difficult for other teams to really check us. With us, it could be our first or second or third or fourth line."

Even when they played poorly they won.

The string ended with a 2-2 tie against Vancouver and a 3-2 loss in Los Angeles, but the Panthers answered that mini-skid with three more victories. Then, just as they had in October, the Cats lost their final game of the month, 2-1, to the Flyers.

A new month brought another new streak. After losing to Pittsburgh to begin the month, the Panthers won five out of their next six in December (a tie with Anaheim was the only blemish). The Panthers were winning at home and on the road. After 30 games, the Panthers were 21-7-2. They were 8-4-0 on the road, 13-3-2 at home. They were 8-3-0 against the rest of the Atlantic Division. They had assumed the best record in the conference on November 3, the best record in the league on November 7. With the exception of the day after the loss to Pittsburgh, they had not relinquished either spot.

Even when they played poorly they won. Game No. 31 was in Uniondale, New York, against the Islanders. Earlier that day, the Isles appointed coach Mike Milbury to be their new general manager. The Panthers welcomed Milbury to his new position with a 3-1 victory that was settled early. Johan Garpenlov scored the quickest goal in team history when he rebounded his own shot past Tommy Soderstrom just 29 seconds into the game. The Panthers got two more goals in the second period to open a 3-0 lead.

"We worked hard and got some good opportunities, and (Mark) Fitzpatrick stood up to the test," Milbury said. "That's how they've been beating not just the New York Islanders, but almost everyone in the National Hockey League."

On the same day the Panthers clipped the Islanders, the Winnipeg Jets made it official that they would take wing and move to Phoenix for the 1996-97 season. While that may seem to have little significance to the Panthers, it did eliminate one of the prominent cities seeking an NHL franchise. If the Panthers were forced to move after the 1995-96 season, there was one fewer choice of sites.

All the talk about selling and moving the team either didn't have any effect on the players, or it spurred them. Two nights after beating the Islanders, they lost to Boston,

but answered that game with three more wins. That did two things. It assured them that they would keep the best record in the league for the 50th day in the last 51. More importantly, it earned a spot for Doug MacLean to be the head coach for the Eastern Conference all-stars in the annual classic in Boston.

"All the staff and all the players are as responsible as I am. I really appreciate what they've done," he said after a victory over New Jersey clinched the job. But he wasn't about to admit that he had won over all his critics. "There were questions when I was hired, and there will be questions now."

There's no question that hockey is a game of tradition. And the Panthers had established one of their own. True to form, they lost their last game of the month (in this case, the last two games) in December and finished the month with an 8-4-1 mark. They still stood 25-10-2,

the second best record in their division and conference, and the entire league.

The last game of the year, in Pittsburgh, was the first game of a seven-game road trip. Bouris, the team's public relations director, used the opportunity to take care of some personal business. He traveled to Long Island to get married. Bouris had spent several years working for Torrey and the Islanders where he met his fiance. When the Panthers took off for two weeks, Bouris tied the knot.

"The team had faxed a congratulatory message to the restaurant where we were having the reception. They gave it to my brother who was my Best Man. The letter was signed by all the guys on the team. To paraphrase, it said, 'It's just like you to take off in the middle of the season when we're getting ready to go on the west-

Lindsay and Barnes celebrated often during the seven-game winning streak (left). Barnes (above) was a fan favorite who drew shouts of "Stuuuuuuuu" when he scored a goal.

coast trip. Enjoy your honeymoon while it lasts because there is a lot of work to be done, because we're going to the Stanley Cup finals.'

"When it was read, everybody was laughing. Bill Torrey was at the wedding, and a few of my old Islanders friends. We knew we had a good team, but to think in December that we were going to be a team, especially in its third year in the league, that was going to go to the finals was unbelievable. But that's the way these guys think. They have so much confidence in their ability. If they play their game, nobody can beat them."

"To be down 6-2 and allow just three shots in the second and third periods because the goaltender was hurt and we had nobody else to put in ... typified the year."

The Panthers finished the seven-game trip 2-3-2, earning both ties in the final two games. If there was one game all season that spoke of their grit, it was the final game of the road trip in Dallas.

The Panthers fell behind, 6-2 heading into the third period. Fitzpatrick had injured himself in practice that morning, so he was unavailable for the game. When Vanbiesbrouck pulled a hamstring during the game, MacLean had nobody to put in in his place, so Beezer had to stay in. "Between periods we talked about the fact that we were getting hammered," the coach recalled. "We talked about Johnny being hurt. Skrudland made a comment about it. All of a sudden, for the second and third

period, we held them to three shots on goal." The Panthers scored four goals in the third period, capped by Stu Barnes' tally with 33 seconds remaining, and escaped with a 6-6 tie.

"To be down 6-2 and allow just three shots in the second and third periods because the goaltender was hurt and we had nobody else to put in, I think sort of typified the year," MacLean said.

"It just seems like we continue to get gutsy performances," Skrudland added. "We never say die."

The Panthers returned home and reeled in the Sharks, 4-1,

in the last game before the all-star game. MacLean was joined in Boston by Vanbiesbrouck and Mellanby. The Beezer had participated before, but it was a first for Mellanby. "It was a huge thrill for me," he said. "It was my 10th year in the league, and I think you kind of get to a point in your career where you don't envision yourself ever having an opportunity like that. That's something that I'll always really, really cherish."

Florida opened the second half of the season on the road with a 1-1 tie at Philadelphia. The next night the Panthers hopped down I-95 to face off with the Capitals. It turned out to be the Johan Garpenlov Show. He recorded the team's first hat trick when he notched his third goal of the game 56 seconds left. The goal lifted the Panthers to a 5-4 win. The Cats also scored four power-play goals, a team record.

The Panthers returned home for a three-game stretch, taking two of three. They lost to Montreal, 6-2, before reversing that score against the Sabres. After defeating Pittsburgh, 2-1, the team hit the road for a return match against Buffalo. How'd they do? Here's a hint: it was the final game of the month. The Sabres scored six times on Fitzpatrick, while the Panthers managed a lone goal by Jovanovski. It was the fourth straight month the Panthers lost their last game and they ended January with a 6-4-3 record.

Still, the Panthers stood 31-14-5, the third best record in the league, second best in their division and conference. After a tie at Boston and a win at Tampa Bay, they led the Atlantic Division and the Eastern Conference, and had

Vanbiesbrouck (left) had saved the Panthers many times in the first three seasons, so they were more than happy to return the favor in Dallas. Garpenlov (above) exploded for the team's first-ever hat trick when he scored thrice against the Washington Capitals.

the second best overall record in the NHL. That set up a major showdown with the Detroit Red Wings, the owners of the best record in the league.

The Wings entered the game 8-0-1 in their last nine games. Certainly, the prevailing thought had to be that the big, bad Red Wings would teach the Panthers a lesson.

The game started poorly for the Panthers. Steve Yzerman scored his second goal of the game just 11:09 into the first period to give Detroit a 3-0 lead. Vanbiesbrouck was pulled. Dvorak and Lowry netted the two goals for the

Panthers, but the Red Wings won, 4-2. The loss dropped the Panthers to second place in the Atlantic behind the Rangers.

"We talked before the game about not showing them too

The Panthers stood third best in the league, second best in their division and conference.

much respect as a team, and then that's just what we did," Mellanby said. If the Panthers wanted revenge, they would have a quick opportunity. Detroit returned the trip to Miami just two nights later, and the Panthers were ready.

"I didn't travel for the game in Detroit," Bouris said. "I watched it on television. I don't think we really had a chance to win, although it was close. They didn't blow us out, which a lot of people were thinking. I'm sure there was the thought, 'This could be the beginning of their end. They'll be exposed tonight.'

"When they got back from Detroit, I sat in and I watched some of the video tape of the game. I watched Doug and Lindy and Duane going over that video tape. I listened to them saying, 'What they do is they like to pass the puck through the neutral zone. If we get our guys just to cover these lanes and cut this off and cut that off...' It was pretty interesting to see if it was going to make any difference.

"Credit our coaching staff, even more credit to our players to adapt in one day. When the Red Wings came into our building, it was a mirror image of the game before. They didn't have a chance to beat us. At that point, I thought, 'I think we're for real now. If we get in the playoffs, which it looks like we're going to, we're going to be tough to beat, because you're going to have to beat us four times out of seven.'"

Billy Lindsay opened the scoring against Detroit with a short-handed breakaway at the 6:02 mark of the first period. Greg Johnson tied it at 10:38, but the Red Wings would score no more. Vanbiesbrouck, who had been pulled from the previous game in the first period, turned back 29 shots. The Panthers were outshot, 30-16, but the Beezer just refused to let any more goals get by him. In the second period alone, Detroit held an 11-1 shots-on-goal advantage. But neither team scored.

Garpenlov gave the Panthers the lead at 10:42 of the third, then Geoff Smith iced the game with just more than three and a half minutes remaining. "It was as good a third period as we've played all year, both ways," MacLean said after the game. "You're always challenged when you play the best team in the league. I thought we responded to the challenge pretty well."

While the Red Wings appeared to be the best team in the Western Conference, the back-to-back match-ups were not a preview of the Stanley Cup Finals. The Wings fell to the Colorado Avalanche, four games to two, in the

the 'Lanche netted three straight goals to send the game to overtime. Then, Mike Keane put the puck past Fitzpatrick 55 seconds into overtime to give Colorado the win. After a 6-4 win over Dallas in which the Cats established a franchise record for wins in a season (34), and a 4-1 win at New Jersey, the Panthers hit the skids.

A 4-0 loss at home to the Rangers started a nine-game winless streak (0-7-2). One of those ties was against Washington, which ironically ended a streak of closing each month with a loss. But the tie also gave the

conference finals. So when the Avalanche traveled to Miami for a game eight days after the Detroit game, the Panthers would find out if they would be able to defeat their future championship opponents. The first game between the two teams ended in a 4-4 tie during the long road trip in January.

This game appeared much better for the Panthers, who jumped out to a 4-1 lead. But

Panthers their first losing month of the season (4-5-3). Included in the winless streak were losses at Buffalo and Hartford, two teams that did not reach the NHL's generous playoff invitation list.

The tide was stemmed partly on the last game of the streak, when the Panthers traveled to

 Garpenlov (left) and Vanbiesbrouck (right) helped the Cats turn the tables on the Red Wings, who had beaten them soundly two days earlier in Detroit.

Madison Square Garden and tied the Rangers, 3-3. They came from behind three times in the game. "It was a big point, like a win," MacLean said afterward.

> **When the final horn sounded in the regular season, there still was hockey left to play.**

Two and three days later, more significant events helped change the course of the team's season. On March 15, the Panthers claimed feisty center Martin Straka on waivers from the Islanders. The next day, they acquired right wing Ray Sheppard and a draft pick from the Sharks for two picks. Both added scoring potential. But nobody knew how quickly the moves would pay off.

In their first game in Panthers sweaters, Straka scored a goal and Sheppard notched an assist as the Panthers ended their nine-game swoon with a 3-0 victory over the Devils. It was the first of three straight wins for the team. Hull scored two goals, giving him 20 on the season, as the Cats beat the Senators, 5-2. Sheppard scored the team's first home hat trick in his third game, a 3-2 victory over the Islanders. The win lifted the Panthers into third place in the conference and only one point out of first in the division.

"The guys made great plays for me," Sheppard said after the game. "Basically I was left alone in front of the net and fortunately they went in."

Unfortunately, the streak ended, and with it, any chance of claiming home-ice advantage throughout the play-offs. Two losses to Tampa Bay, sandwiched around losses to the Rangers and the Penguins left the Panthers in fifth place in the conference. If the season ended then, the Panthers would open the playoffs on the road.

Worse yet, with the second loss to Tampa Bay in four games, Florida finished the month of March with a 3-9-1 mark. After a 3-2 win over Hartford, the Panthers lost two more before a big win on the road.

Meanwhile, at home, there finally was big news. First, Huizenga announced that he would consider selling stock in the team if one owner could not be found. While that was not unheard of in professional sports, it certainly was rare. It meant that the fans in South Florida also could be owners. It also meant that the team would stay in the area forever, if the plan went forward.

Even bigger news, however, was that the Broward County Commission approved a $212 million arena for the team. With the promise of a future NHL all-star game, the Commission reversed its previous decision and agreed to build the arena. A week later, the site was determined in Sunrise.

But while a future in Sunrise meant brighter times for the Panthers, their playoff hopes were beginning to dim, unless they could right their ship. Stuck on 87 points, though they didn't know that 88 would be required to make the tournament, the Panthers needed a boost when they played the Rangers in New York on April 8.

Led by Tommy Fitzgerald's two goals, the Panthers won on the road for the first time since February 21, 5-3. "It was a long time coming," said Fitzgerald, who scored for the first time in 26 games. The victory lifted Florida into a fourth-place tie with Montreal in the Eastern Conference.

The final minutes were agonizing for MacLean. With the team clinging to a 4-3 lead and just 1:17 left, Vanbiesbrouck stopped Adam Graves with a dive. Finally, Lindsay scored an empty-net goal with 15 seconds left to ice the game. "It was the least amount of fun I had in my entire life," MacLean said of most of the final seconds of the game. After Lindsay's goal? "The most fun I ever had."

Three games remained, two at home. The playoff spot was all but assured. The Panthers entertained the Lightning in the first of the three. What could be better than to clinch the berth against your in-state rival? Who knows. The Panthers let a one-goal lead get away, falling 2-1. But the Flyers beat New Jersey, 5-1, and the Panthers first trip into post-season was a reality.

"It was disappointing to lose," Mellanby said. "It dampens the mood."

But Vanbiesbrouck relished the moment more. "It means a lot to the players, but more-so to the franchise and the fans who didn't allow us to move."

There still were two games remaining. Although they were not needed to reach the playoffs, they still were not meaningless. Wins could make the difference in traveling to their first playoff game or staying at home.

The Islanders, who claimed the final spot in the Panthers' first attempt at the post-season in 1994, hosted the Panthers in the first game. Stu Barnes tied the score with 5:00 left in the third period as the teams skated to a 1-1 tie.

The finale was at home against the Rangers.

An inspired effort gave the Panthers a 5-1 win. Five different players scored, Vanbiesbrouck made 18 saves and the Panthers finished the season 25-12-4 at home. Their overall record was 41-31-10, good for fourth best in the Eastern Conference. A first-round series against the Boston Bruins would follow, with the first two games on home ice.

But most importantly, for the first time in team history, when the final horn sounded in the regular season, there still was hockey left to play.

Picking up Straka (left) proved pivotal for the Panthers' late-season surge, which meant the Beezer and his teammates would have to wait a little longer for their summertime rest.

The Florida Panthers began their fourth season with a home game against the Boston Bruins on April 17, 1996. Actually it was the "second season" of their third season, which makes it the fourth season, sort of. Hey, this is new territory, okay?

The well-seasoned Panthers, making their first appearance in the quest for Lord Stanley's Cup, squared off against the Bruins, who were making their 29th straight appearance in post-season, a professional sports record.

The Panthers entered the playoffs trying to regain momentum, while the Bruins probably were the NHL's hottest team. They had won 13 of their last 16 games to move from 10th place in the conference—and out of the playoffs—to fifth, one point behind the Panthers.

But in the playoffs, everybody starts at the same point, a fact that didn't escape the Panthers. "The Bruins could have been saying, 'We went 13-3; where did that go? They took that away from us. Now we've got to start all over again,'" said Greg Bouris, the Panthers' public relations director through the middle of the 1996-97 season. "On the other hand, after a great 60 games and a poor 10 games, we had regained our confidence with a fairly decent 14 games to finish the season.

"Because of the character on this team, the thinking was, 'Okay, we're in. Now let's show them.'"

Since most of the Panthers were picked up from other teams, many of the players had experienced the playoffs before. Brian Skrudland had tasted champagne from the Stanley Cup as a rookie member of the 1986 Montreal Canadiens. This time, he wasn't taking anything for granted. "I was a little igno-

rant of the fact of where I was," he said. "I understood what we were playing for last year. I think I enjoyed it a lot more."

Gord Murphy, who also played in the playoffs in his rookie year (1989) with Philadelphia, knew that the Panthers had just begun to feel pressure. "We put pressure on ourselves," he said. "We proved we could compete in the regular season, and people would say, 'We took you for granted this night or that night.' But in the playoffs, it steps up a notch, and it's another time where careers are made. We wanted to go out and show that we could play at that level and at that intensity. I thought that every guy stepped it up and did an outstanding job."

Finally, game time arrived. All the anticipation, much like the inaugural game fewer than 36 months before, crested inside all who were involved. "That was a fun night," Huizenga said. "It was very exciting. There was a big question mark about how far we would go. Would there be the thrill of victory that compensated for the fear of defeat? So it was a great night, no doubt about it. The arena gets wild, and it did that night."

Once the action started, the Panthers went wild on the Bruins. Ray Sheppard scored the first playoff goal in franchise history—and the first in a playoff game in the state of Florida—at 7:37 of the first period. That just seemed to ignite the team, because while Sheppard's goal was being announced to the Panthers faithful, Mike Hough scored 25 seconds later, giving the Cats a 2-0 lead. Not enough? Fifty-two seconds later, Jody Hull gave the Panthers a 3-0 lead that would be enough.

Rick Tocchet scored two goals to cut the lead to 3-

The pinnacle

 The rats continued to pour down as the Panthers dusted three tradition-rich franchises—the Boston Bruins, the Philadelphia Flyers and the Pittsburgh Penguins—on the way to the Finals.

2, but Jason Woolley answered and Sheppard scored on the power play less than four minutes later and the lead again was three goals.

The Panthers, who had scored five goals in their final regular-season game, had accomplished the trick only one other time dating back to February 18, nearly two months earlier. And they had done it against Bill Ranford, who had entered the playoffs as one of the league's hottest keepers.

The second game was much more physical than the first ... 72 minutes in penalties assessed in the first period alone.

But it was John Vanbiesbrouck who sizzled in the opener. He turned back 42 of Boston's 45 shots, a precursor of things to come for the Cats' netminder. "To be quite candid, they had a lot of good chances," he said after the game. By the time the final horn sounded, the Panthers owned a 6-3 victory, the first—of many—playoff win in franchise history.

The Panthers had plenty of time to enjoy the opener. A Garth Brooks concert, which required a couple of days to set up and take down the stage, had been booked for Miami Arena before anybody realized the Panthers would have a chance to be hosting the opening games of a playoff series. Five days later, the two teams reclaimed the arena for Game 2.

Theme alert. For most of the rest of this chapter, you will read how the "experts" begrudgingly gave the Panthers credit for their accomplishments each step along the way, then brought a reality check, stating the party was over.

Take Game 2, for example. The upstarts certainly were going to revel in their first victory and forget to show up for the second contest, while the Bruins, those guys who own time-share every spring in a condo on "Playoff Road," would regain their edge and flick the Cats away.

Six-two. As in six goals, to just two. As in total domination. But it was the Panthers who again took total control of the game, and the series. Dave Lowry scored twice, Sheppard got three points for the second straight game and Vanbiesbrouck stopped 37 more shots as Florida claimed a 2-0 lead in the series.

The second game was much more physical than the first, as attested by the 72 minutes in penalties assessed in the first period alone. But the Panthers answered the Bruins' charges with goals. Ed Jovanovski scored the first goal at 6:15 of the first. Sheppard made it 2-0 early in the second before Ray Bourque cut the lead to 2-1 three and a half minutes later.

Lowry scored twice in a little more than three minutes in the second period to open up a close game. After Boston cut the lead to 4-2, Woolley and Johan Garpenlov scored for the final margin. And while everybody on both sides knew there was plenty of hockey left to be played, there was little doubt who controlled their fate.

"The series is a long way from over," Bruins coach Steve Kasper said. "Obviously, a tall task is ahead."

Game 3 was in Boston, where the Bruins owned a .650 all-time winning percentage. The Fleet Center holds 17,565 for hockey, which appeared to be just the tonic the Bruins would need to turn the series around. With 2,643 of those patrons disguised as empty seats, the Panthers took the game—and probably the series—away from the B's.

Hull scored 30 seconds into the game on a feed from Fitzgerald. Scott Mellanby made it 2-0 and Hough made it 3-0 all in the first period. The Bruins managed to cut the final score to 4-2 (Hull

 The Panthers proved they were no pussycats against the Bruins. They stood their ground when it was necessary, and they usually answered Boston punches for Florida goals.

scored again for Florida's final goal, giving the Panthers a 4-0 lead), but *The Miami Herald* headline said it all: "BRUINS IN RUINS."

While the Bruins did not have an answer for Vanbiesbrouck, who stopped 40 shots, or the suddenly high-scoring offense of the Panthers, Boston's fans did have an answer to the rats thrown on the ice after Panthers goals in Miami. With the final minutes ticking away,

the first period when Adam Oates beat Vanbiesbrouck low. After Billy Lindsay tied the score at 2:49 of the second period, the Bruins scored the next three goals to take a 4-1 lead into the third period. Vanbiesbrouck was pulled and MacLean was ejected in the second period, and the Panthers left Boston with a 3-1 lead in games, but with a sense of urgency surrounding Game 5.

they showered the ice with garbage, delaying the game and telling their team exactly what they thought of their play.

Those "experts" finally had it right. There was no life in the Bruins, their fans hated them, the Panthers could have carried brooms instead of sticks into the arena for Game 4, because they would need them after the game anyway, winning the series in a sweep.

Boston 6, and Florida 2. So much for the experts. Boston took its first lead of the series in

Final minutes ticking away, Boston fans showered the ice with garbage, delaying the game and telling their team exactly what they thought.

"As far as I'm concerned, our backs are against the wall. We need Game 5," Skrudland, the team's captain, said.

Game 5 was back at home in cozy Miami Arena. While the Bruins still had a large hill to climb, if they won in Miami, they would return home down just 3-2. A win on home ice would put all the pressure on the young Panthers to win a Game 7 in their first playoff series. Both teams had pressure. Both teams had a strong reason to win the game. It should have been a close one. Finally, the game lived up to the billing.

The Panthers won, 4-3, and were airborne. Not just to Philadelphia for the second round. Lindsay's gravity-defying goal late in the third period summed up the series, and maybe the season for the Cats. Let's set the stage.

Skrudland and Paul Laus gave the Panthers a 2-0 lead before the midpoint of the first period, and the Panthers seemed to cruise. But

into the Bruins end. Future Hall-of-Famer Bourque was the lone defender in Lindsay's way. Lindsay faked inside then went outside and got by Bourque. Lindsay turned Bourque completely around, and Bourque's only

Ted Donato scored to make it 2-1 at the end of one period. Jozef Stumpel tied the score at the 9:33 mark of the second, and once again it was a game.

Lowry scored with 3:18 left in the second period to give the Panthers a one-goal lead, but again, Boston came back to tie the score.

With five minutes remaining and an overtime looming—the Panthers were 0-3-10 in the extra period during the regular season—Lindsay grabbed the puck and headed

chance was to trip Lindsay and set up a Panthers power play.

The trip was successful, but the power play was unnecessary. Lindsay, parallel to the ice, slipped the puck past Ranford, and the Panthers had a 4-3 lead.

"Bill Lindsay really illustrates the type of series this was—a hard-working series," Skrudland said after the game. Lindsay down-

The Panthers had Bill Ranford (left) reeling in the series, scoring 16 goals in their four games against the Bruins' top goaltender. Scott Mellanby and the Panthers took their lumps in the physical series, but in the end they escaped with a 4-2 series victory over the B's.

played it. "Ray Bourque is one of the best defensemen in the game and he plays so much, sometimes at the end of the period, you can take a step on him."

General Manager Bryan Murray called the goal, "the biggest goal, maybe, in the franchise history."

Bouris agreed, and describes why. "We're a young franchise, so I think there was this fragile inner psyche. 'Okay, we went through this all year. Here comes the swoon. Here come the Bruins. Here comes Rick Tocchet. Here comes Bill Ranford. Here come Ray Bourque. Here comes Adam Oates.' I think there was the thought that if we lost Game 5 at home, we'd go to Boston up three games to two. They would win that game, and we'd come home to Game 7. 'Oh, forget it.'

So many of the Canadian hockey fans—and some of the media, as well—adopted the Panthers as their team.

"Lindsay went in the air, Ranford came out, challenging Billy on his way down. In mid-air he gets a shot off that goes between the legs of Ranford and in the net. It was a classic, classic moment. That was it. The game and the series were over."

The Panthers had reason—and time—to celebrate. They were the first team to clinch their first-round series, so they waited to find out whom they would play in round two. An interesting sidelight occurred, too. Montreal, Winnipeg, Vancouver and Toronto were the only Canadian teams in the playoffs. Each of them lost in the first round. But Canada is a hockey-crazy country. So many of the Canadian hockey fans—and some of the media, as well—adopted the Panthers as their team.

"We became Canada's team, CBC radio adopted us," Bouris said. "They did reports

about our team. We had a lot of players from Ontario, so the flagship station of the Maple Leafs adopted us as their team. It became bigger than just us; it was bigger than South Florida. We were the sentimental favorite of a lot of people, which is natural. People kind of root for the underdog."

That certainly was the role the Panthers found themselves in for the second series. Not only did they not own home-ice advantage, they were playing the team with the best record in the Eastern Conference, the Philadelphia Flyers. The "Broad Street Bullies" of the 70s had reappeared at the Spectrum, a building that would see its last action in the spring of 1996.

The Flyers were big, strong, aggressive, intimidating, confident and heavily favored. They were right where the Panthers wanted them.

"The Flyers were the big dragon for us in the playoffs last year," Vanbiesbrouck said. "They were the No. 1 team, the team that was going to go all the way, the team that had all the big players. I thought it was a David and Goliath story."

The strength of the Flyers was supposed to be their offense. The "Legion of Doom" line, with Eric Lindros, John LeClair and Mikael Renberg, struck fear in the hearts of defenses. But in Game 1, the Panthers shut them down. Plugged 'em right between the eyes. The Flyers managed only 18 shots on goal—Lindros didn't get any—the entire evening, and only one of them was a tough save for Vanbiesbrouck.

Stu Barnes and Lowry tallied goals for the Panthers, who chalked up their first playoff shutout in franchise history. "I thought we had

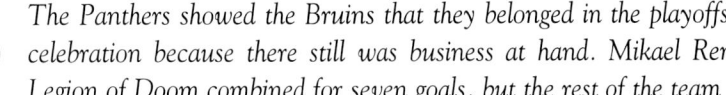

The Panthers showed the Bruins that they belonged in the playoffs, but there was no big celebration because there still was business at hand. Mikael Renberg (above) and the Legion of Doom combined for seven goals, but the rest of the team netted only four more.

We had three guys that game who were sent off for stitches.

a great performance by our defensemen in all aspects," MacLean said. "Robert Svehla and (Terry) Carkner were real horses. They were strong in the defensive zone and strong in the neutral zone playing up on people."

Unlike the Bruins, who rolled over most of the first series, the Flyers were ready for Game 2. To be more accurate, Lindros was ready, and he proved it.

The Panthers cried "Foul!" when Lindros used his stick to inflict pain on Jovanovski, Svehla, Laus, Barnes and Vanbiesbrouck. He sent Jovanovski to the bench with knee spasms. He opened a cut above Barnes' eye. He knocked the mask off Vanbiesbrouck.

But Lindros did other damage with his stick. He finally got off some shots. He

scored one goal and assisted on the other two, as the Flyers evened the series with a 3-2 victory.

"Eric took it into his own hands," Bouris said. "Sticks were flying. We had three guys that game who were sent off for stitches. Guys were losing teeth. And nothing was called. We didn't like that."

The Panthers and their fans were ready for a war as Game 3 approached. "Broad Street Butcher is ours for the hating," one headline read. "Panthers' Most Wanted visits Florida" was a four-column headline. "Panther Enemy No. 1" screamed a third. One of the stories described him as "big, mean, strong and quick," while another described his game as "Cuisinart style."

The players were more focused on stopping his scoring than criticizing his perceived cheap-shots. "We showed in Game 1 that if we get a 20-man effort, we can win," Barnes said. "That's all that we should be thinking about right now."

During the break between Games 2 and 3, Murray received the news that he was named *The Sporting News* executive of the year in the NHL in a close vote over team president, Bill Torrey. But Murray, who was grilled by the media and the fans for firing Roger Neilson at the end of the previous season, did not gloat nor brag. "Anytime anybody off the ice gets any recognition, it has to do with the players," Murray said. "Obviously, bringing Doug and the coaching staff in had a lot to do with it."

MacLean finished tied for second with Tampa Bay's Terry Crisp for coach of the year. Detroit's Scotty Bowman won the award. Jovanovski finished third in the rookie of the year balloting.

The Panthers and the Flyers squared off for Game 3 with all the attention on the Flyers and their rough style of play. But it was a costly penalty for high sticking against Skrudland that largely determined the outcome. Skrudland was in a faceoff with Rod Brind'Amour in the first period. Skrudland tried to anticipate Brind'Amour's movement and instead caught the Flyers center in the face with his stick.

Skrudland was called for a double-minor and the Flyers capitalized. Dan Quinn put in a rebound to give the Flyers a 1-0 lead. Since there was time left in the first penalty, Skrudland remained in the box to serve the second. Fifty-four seconds later, Lindros fired a shot past Vanbiesbrouck for a 2-0 lead.

That lead appeared insurmountable, because the Panthers just couldn't get many shots off. The Flyers outshot them, 17-2 in the

first period and 34-25 overall. Skrudland, who said he tried to read Brind'Amour's move and missed, didn't blame the loss on his penalty, but he did accept a lot of the blame for not being able to come back. "Two shots in a period is not acceptable," he said. "It's not playoff hockey."

"We've got to play better Thursday," Barnes

added. "After the first period, we gathered ourselves, but we never really progressed from there."

The 3-1 loss left the Panthers down two games to one. It was the first time they ever trailed in a playoff series, and it was against a team that was favored to roll over them. Only

Stu Barnes (left) got off his shot enough to lead the team with six points in the series, but not without taking a few shots from Eric Lindros and the Flyers. Skrudland's double-minor gave the Flyers a four-minute power play in Game 3 that helped them to a 3-1 victory.

John Vanbiesbrouck

Ask any personnel man in the NHL. Ask any coach. Ask anybody who knows hockey. You'll get the same response. The Florida Panthers would not have gotten to the Stanley Cup finals in 1995-96 without John Vanbiesbrouck.

"Johnny really had a tremendous year for us," coach Doug MacLean said. "He battled through some adversity part way through the year. He's an up-front guy, a quality person, a great family-man. What he did in the past for us speaks for itself. In the playoffs, he raised his play to another level and was fantastic."

Vanbiesbrouck carried the team throughout the post-season. After a season in which he had a 2.68 goals against average in 57 games, he started all 22 games in the playoffs. He improved his GAA to 2.25, which was best in the playoffs.

"We don't have stars, and John is a star," general manager Bryan Murray said. "John is so strong now. He is so comfortable with himself, so comfortable in the net, so completely in control, that it rubs off on the team."

Vanbiesbrouck doesn't see himself as such. When asked why his face is always the one that appears on screen when ESPN is previewing a Panthers game, he said, "I think they like my mask. It's very artsy.

"I don't think it's known yet, but I think the maturity of this team is happening right in front of everybody. We are interchangeable parts. They could put a Brian Skrudland on the screen. They could put Ed Jovanovski on the screen. We're becoming a very versatile team. When you play a team that you don't know what you're going to get from each line, it's tough to predict. Colorado became the best team in the league last year, because every line scored for them or chipped in, or did something. Then they counted on their big guys who were on top in scoring. Well, we count on certain individuals in this room. They might not get the same recognition, because the points aren't on the board, but they're there in our minds."

But the other guys in the locker room know of his value. And they appreciate his humility. "We work hard as a team," Tom Fitzgerald said. "When I say team, we don't have any individuals here. We don't have any superstars. John Vanbiesbrouck is a so-called superstar, but then again, he's not. He's a down-to-earth guy. He knows that he is a piece of the puzzle here—a big piece, obviously—but he's a piece."

Simply put, Vanbiesbrouck is a superstar on the ice, and a super person off the ice. He credits a lot of his personal growth to his Christian faith. "My faith has become more important to me in the last few years than it ever has been," he said. "I wanted to have a fulfilled feeling inside of me, and that gives me a sense of fulfillment that I've never felt before. And it's a family fulfillment. It's something that is so crucial now that it's my guide.

"It makes you think of positive things. It makes you do positive things. It makes you react positively. In a world of negatives, it helps you out. In times of trouble, you're always calling on your faith in God. One of the biggest factors is it taught me to believe in everybody even stronger. I had a strong belief in my teammates. I had strong belief in my wife, in my family, my in-laws, my parents, but my faith has made that stronger."

Vanbiesbrouck is solid. He's a solid family man, dedicated to spending as much time with his wife and children as his schedule will allow. He's solid between the pipes. He's a solid leader.

"When you have a goaltender who can make the save that is supposed to be made, and then go beyond that, he gives a confidence to the group that you otherwise couldn't have," Murray said. "There are lots of teams, or lots of groups that try to be teams, but because of the lack of goaltending, they just can't win on a regular basis. Our team wins because John is what he is, and he's gotten better. He got better the latter part of last year and in the playoffs and this year he is a better goaltender than he was last year. He shares that with his team. The players trust him, and I think that word in itself is critical to developing an elite program."

Okay, if Vanbiesbrouck is that good, why was he available for the Panthers to select in the expansion draft? Remember that each team could protect just one goaltender for the

draft. Vanbiesbrouck was a member of the Rangers, who also had a younger goalie named Mike Richter. The Rangers saw Richter as the future of the franchise, a decision that certainly proved wise when Richter was a key element of the Rangers' 1994 Stanley Cup championship.

The team didn't want to lose someone of Vanbiesbrouck's abilities with no compensation, so they traded him to Vancouver. The Canucks had Kirk McLean, another young goalie who ironically led his team to the finals against the Rangers in 1994. The Beezer was the odd man out. While Richter and McLean are outstanding goaltenders, Vanbiesbrouck has been the Panthers for four years. That's why his picture is on ESPN's screen.

"The foresight of (New York's and Vancouver's decision) is connected with age," Vanbiesbrouck said. "A lot of the managing in this business falls into catagories. If it's not height and weight, it's age and shoe size. I was older than Mike in New York, and I was older than Kirk in Vancouver, so I don't think it was the worst decision that both teams made. But I don't really think that they knew what was inside of me and what I wanted to give and what I had to give, and what I'm going to continue to give."

● *From the first time he stepped onto the ice for the Panthers, Vanbiesbrouck was a hit. He's represented the team in the all-star game three times and always brings the fans to their feet.*

time would tell how they would respond.

Game 4 was critical. With two of the last three games in Philadelphia (with the dreaded "if necessary" after two of them), the Panthers could not afford to lose another game at home and fall behind, three games to one.

The situation was further compounded because Rob Niedermayer had been in a slump throughout the playoffs. He had not scored a goal and had just one assist through the first eight games. Mellanby, his normal line partner on the right wing, had one goal and one assist, and Garpenlov had two goals and no assists. Not the production you want from your first line, even when you do rely on each line to pick up the scoring.

So MacLean broke up the

line, putting Niedermayer with Martin Straka and Radek Dvorak, and had Tom Fitzgerald take Niedermayer's center spot on the line with Mellanby and Garpenlov.

It didn't take long for the switch to pay dividends. Niedermayer deeked Eric Desjardins at center ice and flew into the Flyers zone uncontested. He put the puck past Ron Hextall to give the Panthers a 1-0 lead at the 1:05 mark of the first period. He then made it 2-0 during a five-on-three advantage.

The second period nearly ended scoreless, but three goals in the final four minutes changed the complexion. The Flyers cut the lead to 2-1 on a goal by Renberg with 3:42 left in the period, followed by Brind'Amour's

"We have debris" in the form of hundreds of rats being showered onto the ice after the Panthers took a 2-0 lead in Game 6 (left). Rhett Warrener (above) and the other youngsters on the Panthers played a key role in the Panthers' run to the Stanley Cup Finals.

No team in its third season was supposed to dispose of the top-seeded team in the conference.

goal 1:18 later to tie it. But Barnes gave the Panthers a 3-2 lead with just five seconds left in the second.

The third period was tight, with no scoring until near the end. But with 1:07 left, Renberg scored his second goal of the game to silence the crowd. That meant the

was tied, two games apiece.

Niedermayer, whose two goals came on his first two shots, said, "It's something that I tried to concentrate on. You don't score if you don't shoot. It felt great getting that first one. It had been such a long time."

Lowry, the soft-spoken left wing, didn't have much to say about his heroics. He did all his talking on the ice, leading the team in scoring throughout the playoffs with 10 goals and

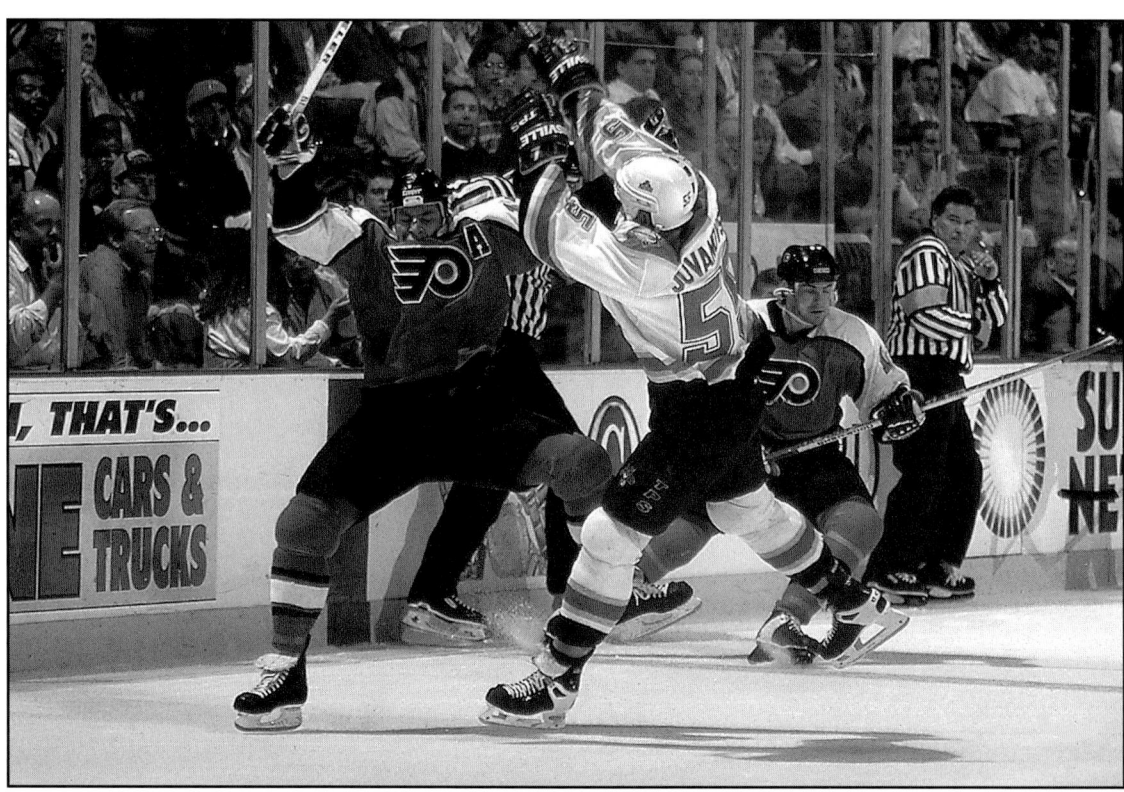

Panthers, who had not played a game in overtime in the playoffs, and had won just two overtime games (out of 46) in their history, had to win in the extra session to avoid going down, 3-1.

But there was no quit in this team. Four minutes into the overtime, Jovanovski, who had given the puck away at center ice before Renberg's goal, fired a shot from long range. Lowry deflected it into the net and the series

17 points. He also led by example, sort of.

Lowry stopped shaving at the start of the playoffs, conjuring up images of old-time hockey players. Playoff beards used to be a tradition in the NHL, though few players grow one with so many games on television. Lowry decided to lend a little tradition to the neophyte franchise.

"That was just an excuse for however long not to shave," he joked. "You look back at the old pictures of the teams that won the Cups and they all had them. It seems to be losing its focus now. I think there were only a couple of guys last year (in the league) who had one, but the game is traditional. It's about history. You just try and keep little things like that going."

Beards aside, the Panthers' confidence grew knowing that the series could not end in Philadelphia.

Game 5 started ominously for Florida. Just 2:27 in, Laus received a five-minute major for elbowing. A major penalty does not end with an opposing goal, which meant the Panthers special teams had to hold on for the full five minutes. They did.

The Flyers did not score during the power play and managed just

two shots against Vanbiesbrouck. "It was a big start for us to kill it off," Rhett Warrener said. "We've been concentrating on that because they got a few goals the last few games."

Fitzgerald described the method the Panthers used to kill the penalty. "You kill two minutes first. Then you kill one minute. Then you're facing a regular two-minute power play." The system worked and the two teams still were scoreless.

The Flyers took a one-goal lead into the third period, but Barnes tied the score. The first overtime was scoreless, but was dominated by the Flyers. The Bullies outshot Florida, 17-5, but could not get the puck past Vanbiesbrouck. Finally, at the 8:05 mark of the second overtime, Mike Hough took a pass and beat Hextall with a wrist shot from the left of the goal mouth to give the Panthers a 2-1 victory, a two-game winning streak (both in overtime) and most importantly, a 3-2 lead in the series returning home.

Lindros had had enough. The upstarts had taken this thing too far. He knew that no team in its third season was supposed to dispose of the top-seeded team in the conference. It would have to end.

"We're coming back here (to Philadelphia)," he stated. "We're going to win." It was locker room wall material for the Panthers.

Nobody would have blinked had Lindros suggested that Game 6 would be close. Through the first five games, Florida held an 11-10 edge in goals. The largest margin of victory in the series was two goals, and the last two games had taken an extra 32:11 to complete.

 Although Jovanovski (left) was engaged in a fierce battle with Lindros, anyone wearing orange was fair game. Lowry (above) sported a playoff beard throughout the post-season.

Fortunately, he didn't predict a close game. Oh-for-two doesn't look good. The Panthers walloped the Flyers, 4-1, to clinch the series.

Even Clarke admired what the Panthers accomplished, and though somewhat begrudgingly, accepted some of the credit.

The scoring started slowly. Lindsay got it started with a short-handed effort at 14:54 of the first period. Lindsay intercepted a pass in front of the Panthers bench and fired a shot past Hextall. No one scored in the second period, but Niedermayer made it 2-0 at 2:55 of the third. Lowry added another goal at 11:12 to give the Panthers a 3-0 lead.

Meanwhile, Vanbiesbrouck was stellar. The Flyers fired 22 shots in the first two periods without once getting one past the Beezer. "He was there whenever they cracked," Lindros said after the game.

The Flyers finally scored with 4:17 left, but by then the Panthers were in total control. When Garpenlov scored an empty-netter with 1:25 left, the final margin was settled.

"We didn't get much respect from the first game we played, and we still don't," Laus said. "We weren't supposed to be in the playoffs. Maybe this will silence the critics."

"We slayed the big dragon," Vanbiesbrouck said. "It showed the fight that this team has, and the resiliency and all those great words you can put up on walls."

For Huizenga, it was better than the first series, because it was the Flyers. "It was special because Bobby Clarke was there," he said. "They were big and tough and they played the Bobby Clarke style. Clarke was no pussycat when he played. You'd see pictures of him with his teeth out. The Flyers tried to beat you up and knock you down. That's all there was to it. For our guys to come away from that was extra

sweet, especially after (Flyers chairman and governor Ed) Snider stole Bobby back."

Even Clarke admired what the Panthers accomplished, and though somewhat begrudgingly, accepted some of the credit. "I certainly would have liked to beat them," he said. "But I was happy for the players that I had brought in there, because they were my friends, and I liked them. They were good people. I know how hard they worked, and I was happy for the organization. They had done things right, and they had had some success. There are no guarantees in this business that you're going to be successful every year. But that organization is a good organization, and they're going to be successful.

"I don't know if bittersweet is the correct

word. In sports, you're going to run into these kinds of things along the way if you move around a bit. To go against them was good. I think it was terrific for the sport. We had Lindros and a pretty good team. They had a pretty good team, and it was a good series, I think."

Okay, the Panthers had won their first series, which should have been enough. Then, they went out and bullied the Bullies and won their second series, becoming just the second team in NHL history to advance to the conference finals in its third season. Surely, the run would end against the mighty Penguins. Think again.

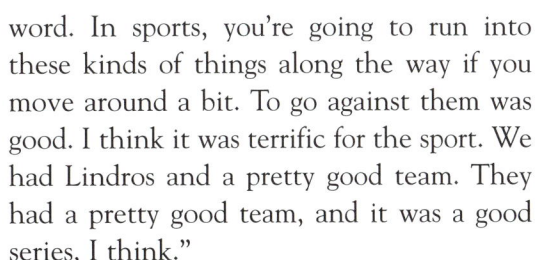

The National Hockey League tradition of a post-series handshake (left) quickly became a popular one for the Panthers, who became the third team in league history to win their first two playoff series, prompting a less-organized but equally rewarding celebration (above).

GRIT and Glory

The Penguins had defeated the Rangers, four games to one. In the final game, both Mario Lemieux, who led the NHL in scoring with 161 points (69 goals, 92 assists), and Jaromir Jagr, who was second with 149 points (62, 67), scored hat tricks. The Pens led the NHL with 362 goals (4.4 per game) during the regular season.

"They're a highly talented team. They've got all the firepower and they really showed it in the first two series," defenseman Gord Murphy said. "We don't want to get into any run-and-gun style with any club. We don't feel that's very good for our chances."

Game 1 in Pittsburgh belonged to the Panthers. Lowry and Fitzgerald each scored twice and Mellanby added another goal as the Cats won, 5-1.

Lowry had been hot throughout the playoffs. He had been dubbed "Midas" by his teammates for his golden touch. He was so hot that he scored his two goals on *zero* shots. One goal went in off a defender's skate and the other went off the goalie's stick. Both were attempted passes.

Lowry tried to deflect the praise just like he had "deflected" 10 goals during the playoffs, fourth highest in the league. "A lot of

While the Penguins averaged 4.2 goals during the previous round of the playoffs, the Panthers advanced without scoring more than four goals in any game. They averaged 2.5 goals per game, down from 3.1 per game in the regular season.

But the Panthers were on a roll. And each of their four games with the Penguins during the regular season was a one-goal game, with the Pens winning three. So, guardedly, the Panthers entered the series as a confident group.

"No matter what happens in this series, our confidence is going to stay high," MacLean said.

the goals haven't been pretty," he said. "But in the playoffs, you go to the net and try to bury it. (Linemates Stu Barnes and Ray Sheppard) make you a better player. There's no pressure playing with them. Ray is a natural scorer and Stu's an offensive playmaker with great speed. All they wanted me to do was go to the net, go to the corner and get the puck. If you go to the net with those guys, you're bound to get opportunities."

The Panthers got most of the opportunities in Game 1, and when the Penguins got one, the Beezer stopped it. Vanbiesbrouck turned back 32 shots in the game as the Panthers held Lemieux and Jagr pointless. It was just the fourth time all season that had happened, and the first time in Pittsburgh.

But the Penguins were not worried. They had not won the first two games of a playoff series in more than three years, so they were in a comfortable situation being down, 1-0.

Lemieux came back in Game 2 and combined with goalie Tom Barrasso to lift the Penguins to a 3-2 victory. After a scoreless first period, Lemieux missed the first half of the sec-

one goal 29 seconds into the third period, but Lemieux answered that with a goal of his own at 8:12 to stretch the lead to 3-1. Lindsay then scored at the 12:19 mark

Lowry had been dubbed "Midas" by his teammates for his golden touch.

and the Cats were down by just one. But Barrasso stopped Lindsay on a breakaway with less than three and a half minutes remaining.

ond period with a bout with the flu. But in his first shift of the period, he gathered in a loose puck, slid it across the crease to Jagr, who punched it past Vanbiesbrouck for a 2-0 lead. Sergei Zubov had given the Penguins a 1-0 lead on a power-play goal earlier in the period.

Sheppard brought the Panthers to within

The Panthers knew they could be in a better position. "We're not satisfied with what happened," Fitzgerald said. But they had earned a split on the road, the goal for most teams in the first two games of a series

Mellanby (left) continued to be a major factor, scoring the first goal of a Game 1 victory at Pittsburgh, as well as a goal in Game 6 to help keep the Panthers alive. Lowry (above) led the Panthers in scoring in the playoffs, matching his regular-season total of 10 goals.

that opens away from home. And Game 3 was back home in the "Rats' Nest."

The Panthers had established themselves as a team that played tough, tight defense with outstanding goaltending, then tried to take advantage of a few scoring opportunities to slip by the opposition in a low-scoring affair. Game 3 shot that theory full of holes. Trailing 2-1 in the second period, Dvorak scored his first goal in three months to tie the score. (Dvorak had been slashed across the face—cutting his lip and losing three teeth—but returned to the action to knot the game.)

Game 3 was back home in the "Rats' Nest."

The third period was a science-fiction thriller for Panthers fans. The Cats outshot the Penguins, 23-2 (including 20 straight), in the period to earn a 61-28 edge for the game. The 61 shots were the most in franchise history, and the 23 in the third resulted in three goals (Barnes scored twice for the Panthers and Straka added the final tally) as Florida regained control of the series with a 5-2 victory.

"You don't expect Florida to get 60 shots in a game," Lemieux said. "It was just breakdowns on our part, not playing smart. We just had a bad third period."

Coach Ed Johnston was less diplomatic. "As soon as we got up 2-1, we went into reverse. It was totally inexcusable to play like that. One thing we know, we can't play any worse than we did. We just folded the tent. You only get a handful of opportunities to get this far, and to play the way we did at the end is just (bad words).

"I've been in a lot of playoff games and this is the first time I've ever been in the playoffs where the goalie had to stop 60 shots."

Game 4 reverted to the type of game that the Panthers expected to play: a tight-checking, low-scoring affair decided by one goal. Lowry put the Panthers up 1-0 in the second period, assisted by Carkner and Sheppard. After two periods, the Panthers held a 26-11 advantage in shots, but only a one-goal lead.

That changed at 8:57 of the third when Brad Lauer put back a rebound to tie the score at 1-1. Then, with 3:31 remaining, Bryan Smolinski silenced the crowd with his fifth goal of the playoffs. Smolinski snatched a loose puck after Vanbiesbrouck stopped a shot by

not the end of the world." But the Panthers knew they had let a big chance get away. Instead of heading back to Pittsburgh with a 3-1 lead, they were all knotted up at two games apiece. With home-ice advantage re-established, the Penguins only had to hold serve to move on to the Stanley Cup Finals. Things would only get tougher for the Florida Panthers.

Game 5 was another example of stout defense and flawless goaltending that the Panthers had gotten so used to during this improbable playoff run. The unfortunate thing for the Panthers was that it was Tom Barrasso turning in a Beezer-like effort. He stopped all 28 Florida shots, giving him 60 saves on the Panthers' last 61 shots.

Meanwhile, the Penguins scored a goal in each period, prompting the Pittsburgh fans to shower the ice with toy Penguins. J.J. Daigneault scored on a power-play goal in the

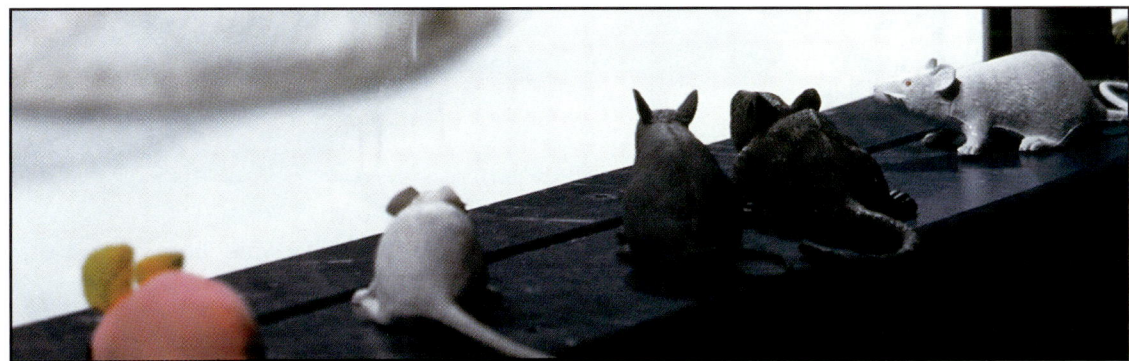

Lemieux. It was the first time during the play-offs that the Panthers had lost a game when they led heading into the third period. They had gone 34-4-3 during the regular season in those situations.

"No problem. We've bounced back from this lots of times," MacLean said after the game. "It's

first, Petr Nedved made it 2-0 in the second and Tomas Sandstrom finished the scoring with an empty-netter.

"Hopefully we'll respond like a rat when he's backed into a corner," said Skrudland, pun

Barnes (left) and the Panthers outshot the Penguins, 23-2, in the third period, outscored them, 3-0, and won the game, 5-2, turning the hockey world upside down, much to the delight of all who watched, including some guests who hardly could wait to get on the ice.

scoring, but if you get good goaltending and have good defense, you can compensate for that."

Huizenga recalls believing the Panthers not only could win Game 6 at home but also Game 7 in Pittsburgh. "At that point, everybody had become believers. We were winning as many games away as we were at home. So we were say-

Sentinel after Game 5. "The only news is when you win four games, and no one's there yet."

No one was there after Game 6 either as the Panthers played inspired hockey in front of the home fans in what most experts thought would be the final time of the season. The Pens took a 2-1 lead into the closing moments of the sec-

When the final horn sounded, the Panthers were one game away from the Stanley Cup Finals ...

ing, 'We've got a shot to win this thing.' It's no secret that if we would have been put away by Philadelphia, no one would have been surprised. We also knew if we got put away by Pittsburgh, that wouldn't be a disgrace. But we were saying, 'Hey, this is possible.'"

Maybe Skrudland summed up the attitude best when he told David Hyde of the *Sun*-

ond period, but Lindsay put it past Barrasso to tie the score. Straka gave the Panthers a 3-2 lead in the third period on a spectacular goal. He slipped past Daignault at the blue line and then passed to Lindsay. Lindsay passed it back and Barrasso went down. Straka flipped it past the Pens' goalie.

Sandstrom tied the score later in the third, but Niedermayer got the game-winner 6:02 left in regulation. When the final horn sounded, the Panthers were one game away from the Stanley Cup Finals, and the fans went nuts. "I've been in

Stanley Cup Finals in Philadelphia, which is a great hockey town," Mellanby said. "I've just never seen craziness for a team like we had last year. It was phenomenal."

While the fans whooped it up through the night and into the next day, the players enjoyed the victory for a few minutes. But they knew that there were still goals to reach. "We have mentioned that we are proud of what we've accomplished," Skrudland said, "but in the same sentence, we realize we haven't won anything yet."

Game 7 would mean the end of somebody's season. Either the mighty Penguins might be saying farewell to Lemieux, who had talked of retirement, or the Panthers magical season would finally die. For one member of the Panthers organization, it brought eerie memories.

Denis Potvin, the team's television analyst,

was a member of the 1975 New York Islanders, who reached Game 7 of the Eastern Conference finals in their third year of existence. But the Islanders fell to the Flyers, who went on to win the Cup.

"It's amazing how the scenario almost repeated itself," he said. "I think what happens is that when you get a team like Pittsburgh, and that's what you count on when you're the underdog, that they might think that they just have to show up and they'll win the hockey game. But the character and the grit that was drafted by the Panthers is really what won that game.

"When everybody says you're down and out, and you're asked by your coach to look into the

mirror and make a decision: 'Are you down and out, or do you have 60 minutes of hockey to play?' Character says, 'To heck with it. This is going to be my 60 minutes, and whatever happens, happens, but I'll give it my best shot.' That's all a coach can ask for.

"The Panthers played just about as good a hockey game as I've ever seen in Game 6. Going into Pittsburgh for Game 7, there was no reason for them to play the way they did, because they could have bowed out and no one would have said anything."

Both teams were ready for this game. Mike Hough scored a goal in the first period to give the Panthers a 1-0 lead, then neither team scored for the rest of two periods. Hough had scored three previous goals in the post-season, and the Panthers were 3-0 in those games. He scored in the first playoff game against Boston

and then two games later to help the Panthers to a 3-0 lead in the series. In the second round, he scored an overtime goal in Game 5 in the last game played at the Philadelphia Spectrum.

"I hadn't gotten my goal for this series, so I thought I'd chip in my one goal and take it from there," he said. The Panthers took that 1-0 lead into the third period because

(Left) Straka was alone in front with the goalie down, and he took advantage, giving the Panthers a 3-2 lead in Game 6. Potvin (above, left) was a member of the third-year Islanders who advanced to Game 7 of the conference finals in 1975. Fitzgerald (above, left) says scoring the game-winning goal in Game 7 is "a moment I'll never forget."

"You kind of had to pinch yourself. You're going to the Stanley Cup finals."

Nedved tied the score early in the third period, but Fitzgerald fired a long shot past Barrasso 4:55 later to put the Panthers ahead

Vanbiesbrouck was spectacular. He turned away 39 of 40 Pittsburgh shots for the game.

tics during the regular season, were at the top during this series.

"Knowing that one more win and you're off to the Stanley Cup Finals was unbelievable," Fitzgerald said. "Some guys may never, ever get there again, and it was just something to be credited with the game-winning goal. It's just something, it's a moment I'll never forget."

for good. Garpenlov added an insurance goal and the Panthers had reached the pinnacle.

The 3-1 victory for Florida was a total team effort. While cliche-ish, it was true. Eighteen of 20 skaters who saw action scored in the series. Lowry, Fitzgerald and Lindsay, who stood in the middle of the team scoring statis-

Defensively, the Panthers shut down Lemieux and Jagr, the two highest scorers in the league during the regular season. The duo was held to one goal each, both in Pittsburgh's Game 2 victory.

"You kind of had to pinch yourself. You're going to the Stanley Cup finals," Niedermayer

said. "You dream of it as a kid, pretend you're playing in the Stanley Cup finals on the ponds in the winter."

These were men, it was spring and there was no pretending. They were going to the Stanley Cup Finals. Several of the players had been in the Finals before, but this was different. For Skrudland, it was the first trip in 10 years. As a rookie, he had earned a ring with the Canadiens, but he learned a lesson on the effort needed to win in the playoffs during a series against the New York Islanders.

The Islanders were a veteran team, while the Canadiens had a bunch of young guys. After an Islanders victory in the Nassau Coliseum, Skrudland was walking by the Islander dressing room and saw players nearing or over 30 covered with ice bags and tape, bruises

and bumps. They didn't say a word. There was no stereo blasting. There was no celebrating. They had paid the price.

Bouris, who worked for the Islanders at the time recalls Skrudland's reaction. "His team had lost. But he looked in that room, and said, 'Something is wrong with this picture. We're the beaten team. We're the team that should be limping out of here.' He realized then that there is a price to pay, and if you're not willing to pay that price, then you're never going to clear the hurdle."

The Panthers did not clear the final hurdle. After a grueling series against Pittsburgh, the Panthers

The Panthers are a close-knit group, whether celebrating another victory or recovering from defeat. They needed that in the Finals against Patrick Roy (above) and the Avalanche. Roy had little success in his first two years against the Panthers, but he was 4-0-1 against them in 1995-96, including a four-game sweep in which he allowed only four goals on 151 shots.

... it came at such an inopportune time, putting the Panthers down, two-zip.

traveled directly to Denver for the first game against the Colorado Avalanche. Colorado had a full week of rest between their Game 6 clincher at home against Detroit and the first game, again at home, in the Finals. The Panthers had two off days between two road games.

and the Avalanche held a series lead it would not relinquish.

Game 2 was a game that the Panthers would just as soon forget. Peter Forsberg scored a natural hat trick and the Avalanche scored four times on the power play in an 8-1 victory2. The eight goals tied a Panthers franchise record for goals allowed and the seven-goal margin set a franchise record.

Maybe the Panthers could be excused for

But don't expect the Panthers to make any excuses. That would be contrary to their character. A hot team with a hot goaltender ran into a hotter team with a hot goaltender.

Colorado won the first game, 3-1. Fitzgerald scored the first goal, but Scott Young, Mike Ricci and Uwe Krupp scored goals in the second period to give Colorado the lead. Patrick Roy turned away 25 shots

appearing to take the night off. A team in its first excursion into the playoffs was playing its 102nd game of the season (111th, counting the exhibition season). But it came at such an inopportune time, putting the Panthers down, two-zip.

Game 3 was critical. Only one team had overcome a 3-0 deficit in games to win the Stanley Cup (Toronto, 1942). If the

Panthers wanted to bring home Lord Stanley's Cup, a win in the Rats' Nest was essential. It didn't happen.

Claude Lemieux, who had missed the first two games of the series because of a suspension from the Detroit series, scored just 2:44 into the first period to give Colorado the lead. Sheppard tied the score six and a half minutes later on a power play. Two minutes later, Niedermayer gave the Panthers a 2-1 lead they

the third period. Maybe it was appropriate that Game 4 was a classic. Two of the best stories in sports in 1996 were bringing their series to a conclusion, and the final chapter would be one to remember. The Panthers, in their third season, were attempting to claim the league championship. The Avalanche, in their first year in Colorado after 16 years in Quebec as the Nordiques, were doing the same.

took into the second period.

But Mike Keane and Joe Sakic each scored in the first three minutes of the second period to give Colorado the lead again. From there it turned into a defensive struggle, as neither team was able to light the lamp. The two squads totaled 11 shots combined in

The first period was scoreless, as was the second, and the third. One overtime came and went without any cause for celebration. The second did as well. The Avalanche wanted to end the series. There was no way any of these

Fitzgerald (left) scored the first goal of the Finals, but it wasn't enough. After carrying the team throughout the playoffs, Vanbiesbrouck (above) struggled against Colorado, at least until Game 4 when he turned away the first 55 shots. Uwe Krupp's shot finally beat him.

players wanted to have to go back home without the trophy in hand. They had seen what the Panthers did with their backs to the wall against Pittsburgh, and they had no interest in seeing if they could do it again.

We're just a bunch of guys who are willing to pay the price, come and play hard every night ... a group of guys where everybody cares for each other.

The Panthers were scratching for survival. This franchise, named for an animal that nearly was extinct, could empathize. So neither side backed down.

Roy was the immovable object. Vanbiesbrouck was the irresistible force. Roy turned away 63 Florida shots, while Vanbiesbrouck stopped 55 attempts by Colorado.

At 4:31 of the third overtime, at 1:06 in the damp Miami morning, Krupp let fly with a slap shot from Vanbiesbrouck's left at the blue line. It handcuffed the Beezer and got by him.

The game—the longest 1-0 game in Stanley Cup Finals history—was over. The series, the season, the Year of the Rat, was

over. Sakic, the Avalanche captain, lifted the Stanley Cup over his head. Skrudland and his mates could only watch. But there were few hung heads.

"You eliminate Game 2 and the rest of those games could have gone either way," Bouris said. "I'm a Panther saying this, so it might be taken with a grain of salt, but I really, truly believe that three of the four that we lost we very easily could have won. The series could have had a different outcome."

Lowry added, "It was disappointing that we didn't win, but to look around the room when it was all done, and to see the guys that you did it with, well, that was special. We are a team without any real superstars, with the exception of Johnny. We're just a bunch of guys who are willing to pay the price, come and play hard every

 Vanbiesbrouck shut down Valeri Kamensky (left), Joe Sakic (top) and the rest of the Avalanche for better than five periods and kept the fans on their feet until the very end.

night, and it's a group of guys where everybody cares for each other. Even from day one, we were written off, and we just kept rolling and rolling. They just kept waiting for us to fall, but we got on a great roll and we rolled it as long as we could."

Even a grizzled veteran of nearly 30 years in the NHL and four Stanley Cup championships had a new perspective. "Obviously you always like to win it all, but it's the first time I could ever say that I didn't feel down after not winning the championship," Torrey said. "The way this team performed—every challenge that was thrown, it met head-on, and any time anybody wrote it off, it rebounded even stronger. Knowing some of these players as long as I have, to see them get the sense of satisfaction out of it was great."

Almost lost in the excitement of reaching the finals was the fact that hockey was secure in South Florida. The arena deal in Sunrise assured fans that the Panthers would be in the area for years to come. Huizenga announced in early June that he would sell public stock in the team while maintaining principal ownership, meaning that stability that most franchises cherish was like the proverbial "biscuit in the basket."

Bouris says all the credit goes to the players.

"I have nothing but admiration for the guys in that locker room," he said. "I admire these guys who were given up for dead by other teams, coming to a new expansion market. A lot of these guys had paid the price. They're not one-year wonders. They paid with a lot of blood and sweat. They left some tears behind in other rinks, a lot of flesh in other arenas.

"And I think it could have been very easy to look at this area that is traditionally perceived as the retirement community of the world, and think, 'OK, these teams, coaches and scouts could be right. I'll go there and hockey will become a lesser priority. I'm going down to Florida and have a little fun. So what if we get beat. We're an expansion team.'

"Teams may go years and may never be able to assemble a group with the amount of pride that this group has. It's an unbelievable bunch. I don't care what anybody else says, it's not because of any ownership, it's not because of any sunshine, it's not because of any marketing, it's not because of any public relations, it's not because of any great coaching skill. It's because of the guys in our locker room that South Florida will have a hockey team for a long time.

"And the way this team plays, whoever puts that sweater on now—although that sweater and that logo is only four years old—is going to have to wear it realizing that the Brian Skrudlands, the John Vanbiesbroucks, the Scott Mellanbys, and the Gord Murphys have set a high standard."

The 1995-96 Florida Panthers fell one stop short of World Champions. In so doing, they set a high standard and high expectations for 1996-97.

The fans showed up en masse at the post-season rally to let Ray Sheppard (left, above) and his teammates that they appreciated them. (Above) Wayne Huizenga addressed them, flanked by the Prince of Wales Trophy to his right and his management staff to his left.

The Florida Panthers entered the 1996-97 season with a new situation: nothing new. For the first time in franchise history, all of their front-office staff members were in the same position they held the previous year.

In the first season, everybody was new. President and Governor Bill Torrey had come from the Islanders, General Manager Bob Clarke had come from the Flyers, and Head Coach Roger Neilson most recently had been with the Rangers. After the first year, Clarke returned to Philadelphia and was replaced by Bryan Murray. After the following season, despite finishing one point out of the playoffs in each of his first two seasons, Neilson was fired and was replaced by Doug MacLean.

That new combination helped the Panthers reach the Stanley Cup Finals in their third season, and no changes were made. Except for the expectations.

The Panthers were picked for next to last or last in the league before their first season. Respectability was the forecast the second year, and after replacing the popular Neilson with the unproven MacLean, doom and gloom again were predicted for Year Three.

Not this time. The Panthers were expected to be good—as long as they kept doing the things that got them to this point. The first priority was re-signing back-up goaltender Mark Fitzpatrick. Fitzy was a free agent, and Murray said that retaining him was the top priority in the off-season. "He has become one of the best No. 2 guys—probably the best—in the league, and it's only because of John Vanbiesbrouck that he can't start here," the general manager said. "He's very good, very competitive, real athletic. He will end up being a No. 1 goaltender, either here or somewhere."

Fitzpatrick was heavily courted by other teams, but he chose to stay with Florida because of his respect for the organization. "It all boils down to the organization—I think it's the best organization in the NHL," he said. "I realize that it probably is hurting my career a bit by not moving on, but I just love the organization, and love my teammates and love our fans here. With all that, it certainly made my choice a lot easier.

"What probably influenced me the most was the closeness of our team, the friendships we have developed over the past three or four years. I'm one of the 12 guys who have been here since day one, and we have been through a lot. We basically were not wanted by other teams out there, so we all had something to prove, and that brought us even closer."

That closeness, and even more, the level of play those original 12 guys had instilled in the entire franchise, had caught the attention of the rest of the league. The expectations also brought extra intensity to opponents who faced off with the Panthers.

'Twas no fluke, or, The year of the knee

The Panthers entered their fourth season with sky-high expectations. They started hot, able to deflect a lot of problems, but finally the injuries caught up with them. They finished fourth in the Eastern Conference, but entered the playoffs with less confidence than the year before.

"Players in the league, coaches in the league, management in the league, they respect the Panthers," head coach Doug MacLean said. "And that's what is important, to be respected by your peers. The Panthers have a tradition that some teams take a lifetime to develop, and that tradition is in place because of a great man-

"It's a tough league, and if you don't play to your potential every night, you have a tough time winning."

One tradition the Panthers have claimed as their own is getting key contributions from every player on the roster. The old cliche, "There is no I in team" is very evident in the Florida locker room. "I think we've got our superstar in the one position that you'd want it. We sort of thrive off John Vanbiesbrouck," Billy Lindsay said. "We've got a lot of good players here, but not many great ones. If you went around the room, you wouldn't say, 'He's a great player,' but we do have a lot of good players, a lot of awfully, awfully good players."

agement team of Mr. Huizenga, Bill Torrey, Bryan Murray and Chuck Fletcher.

"Our core group of players really have set the standard. That really speaks volumes about the people. I've only been a small part of it for a year, but the people who have been here for four years are the ones who have set the standard. We're getting to the point now where teams are going to bring their best game to play us, which is a real exciting challenge.

"It's a tough league, and if you don't play to your potential every night, you have a tough time winning."

Those awfully good players took the ice for the first time for real in a city where they had tasted considerable success the previous year. They had gone 1-0-1 in Philadelphia in the regular season, then won two of three games in the Eastern Conference semifinals. They had won the last game ever played in the old Spectrum, and they were given the opportunity of playing in the first game in the new Core States Center.

Nobody on the Panthers was in a celebratory mood, however. The building didn't matter to them. The Panthers hated the Flyers, and the 143 days since they last played for real hadn't lessened that.

It only took the first half of one period for the first fight of the year to break out—between Paul Laus and Dan Kordic. But it took even less time to net the first goal. The two teams had combined for just 20 goals in 300 minutes of action during the previous regular season, but after 4:04 of the first period, the score stood at 1-1.

"He (Hextall) came flying out and I was kind of surprised to see him standing there almost next to me," Smyth said.

The Flyers answered a short time later when rookie Dainius Zubrus, the youngest player ever to wear a Flyers jersey, flipped a shot toward the goal on an attempted pass, and it

Lindsay deflected a shot from Ed Jovanovski from the point, but was stopped by Ron Hextall. The rebound came out to Brad Smyth, who was parked just outside the crease. Smyth, who had one career NHL goal heading into the season, banged it past Hextall to give the Panthers a 1-0 lead.

ended up bouncing off Vanbiesbrouck's skate for the rookie's first NHL goal.

Scott Mellanby, who broke into the league with Hextall in 1986 with Philadelphia, got a roughing penalty late in the second period

Under the direction of head coach Doug MacLean, the Panthers won or tied their first 12 games. Paul Laus (above) thought being the Panthers' enforcer was a "Capital" idea.

when he crashed into Hextall. The Flyers were not able to capitalize, and when Mellanby bolted from the penalty box, he received a pass from Lindsay and fired it past Hextall for a 2-1 lead.

Keeping with Flyers-Panthers tradition, there was a scrum in front of the Florida net as the clock ticked down. But Vanbiesbrouck turned back two point-blank attempts from Rod Brind'Amour. The Panthers still couldn't clear, but Johan Garpenlov, from his backside, swatted the puck away from Kevin Haller and scored an empty-net goal with eight seconds remaining to seal the victory.

> ## "When the schedule came out in July ... it was a touch nerve-racking."

"When the schedule came out in July, and I saw this opening weekend at Philadelphia and New York, it was a touch nerve-racking," MacLean said. "One down, one to go."

The next one was another home opener, the Madison Square Garden debut of "The Great One"—Wayne Gretzky— in a Rangers uniform.

"High-profile athletes in New York, the media capital of the world, on the cover of *Sports Illustrated*—what could be better?" Torrey said of the newly formed combination of Gretzky and former teammate Mark Messier. "Everybody is falling all over themselves. Plus you have that little controversy of whether they're past their primes."

The season showed that while maybe they had slowed a little bit, they still were a very potent duo. But on this night, the Panthers spoiled their second show in two nights, 5-2. Brian Skrudland and Rob Niedermayer each scored twice and Mellanby added another. Vanbiesbrouck turned back 36 shots and the Panthers were 2-0. In their first three seasons,

the Panthers had not won their opening game, much less their first two. But it was a sign of things to come.

At approximately 7:30 p.m. on October 8, 1996, three years and two days after they took to the ice for the first time, the Florida Panthers unveiled the Eastern Conference championship banner. A sellout crowd of 14,703 roared as the Prince of Wales Trophy was paraded around the ice.

"We'd sure love to be having a Stanley Cup brought out there, too," Mellanby said. "We're working on that. But it's nice, in only three years, to be able to have something like that to

put up in our building. We're all proud of that. At the same time, we've got to drop the puck and get going again."

Of course, there was a hockey game to be played. The Rangers came to town with the Panthers to try to even the score from two nights earlier. Speaking of the scoring, the Panthers did so first, when Tom Fitzgerald beat Glenn Healy with just more than a minute remaining in the first period, and the ice was showered with...nothing.

The NHL had done what Orkin or Miami Arena security could not do. It had kept the Panthers fans from throwing rats onto the ice following Panthers goals. A rule change invoked during the off-season read, "Any concerted or widespread conduct by the fans which results in the littering of the ice with any type of object (except, in the case of a hat-trick, hats) will not be tolerated. A two-minute delay of game penalty may be assessed against the home team."

Rats!

Of course, it also meant that fans could not throw octopi onto the ice after Red Wings goals in Detroit, but Panthers faithful felt the league was picking on them. Still, the Panthers brass let the fans know they would enforce the rule. "Anyone throwing a rat will immediately be ejected," Panthers executive vice president and alternate governor Dean Jordan said. "We can't afford to get power plays called against us."

The Panthers dominated the Rangers during the home opener, much like they had in

A Hall-of-Fame shot (left)? Wayne Gretzky and the New York Rangers brought their star-studded show to Miami to face John Vanbiesbrouck and the Panthers. Jason Woolley (above) found a home with the Cats, before being traded to Pittsburgh with Stu Barnes.

spoiling the Rangers lid-lifter two nights earlier. But this time Healy was as magnificent as Vanbiesbrouck, and the Panthers held only a 1-0 lead throughout the second period and all but the final 32 seconds of the third.

As the final seconds ticked away, Adam Graves scored on a rebound with a backhand shot and the game was tied. The Panthers were frustrated because the Rangers got the faceoff in the Panthers' zone when the linesman called icing.

The Panthers were disappointed with the tie, but still had to feel good about going 2-0-1 in their first three games against the league's elite. And after seeing their banner raised and a highlight video from the previous season, they got to enjoy for one last time their remarkable third season. "It was pretty emotional," Vanbiesbrouck said. "Doug came in before the game and said, 'You guys deserve this. Take a moment and appreciate it.'"

Vanbiesbrouck earned NHL player of the week honors for the first week with a .967 save percentage.

New York's Alexei Kovalev had a chance to stop a clearing pass, but lifted his skate. The official ruled that he had made an attempt to stop the puck. The Panthers did not agree, but it didn't matter.

After the opening three-game stretch, the Panthers got down to the daily grind of an 82-game NHL schedule. The Hartford Whalers were next in town and the Panthers tore into them like Cat Chow. Ray Sheppard and Fitzgerald scored in the first period, Gord Murphy and Lindsay tallied goals in the second, and Mike Hough and Per Gustafsson finished the scoring with goals in the third. The Panthers outshot the Whalers, 32-21, and

Vanbiesbrouck once again was stellar, turning away every Hartford shot in a 6-0 win.

Vanbiesbrouck earned NHL player of the week honors for the first week with a .967 save percentage. After four games, he had given up four goals, only three of them at even strength. "This is something that was accomplished together," he said after hearing the news.

the league. Mark Fitzpatrick was between the pipes for the Panthers, the first start for Fitzy since the next to last game of the regular season (27 games).

The Sharks managed to get three goals by Fitzpatrick, but Murphy, Garpenlov and Dave Lowry scored for Florida as the teams skated to a 3-3 tie. The following night the Panthers had to face off against the defend-

The Panthers then went on a three-game road trip to San Jose, Colorado and Phoenix. They owned an all-time record of 47-45-17 on the road, an outstanding mark for any team, much less an expansion club.

San Jose had made numerous changes in their lineup during the off-season, trying to improve on their 20-55-7 mark which was the second worst in

ing champions, the Colorado Avalanche. MacLean was a little miffed that his team had to be on the ice for a 7 p.m. start when the players didn't arrive in Denver until 3 a.m. But after the game, it would have been hard to tell who was tired.

The Panthers-Rangers rivalry has developed into one of the league's most intense, partly because of former Rangers like Vanbiesbrouck (left) who toil for Florida, but mostly for the knock-them-to-their-knees action and superstars like Messier and Mellanby (above).

Vanbiesbrouck turned away 25 of 26 shots. Garpenlov and Fitzgerald scored for the Panthers, and the Cats had their first win in Denver. Three nights later, they ended their road trip with their perfect record intact after a 1-1 tie in Phoenix.

The Panthers returned home and earned a 5-2 victory over the resurgent Ottawa Senators. It was a repeated theme, as the

Panthers passed the scoring load around. "That's how this team has been successful over the past three or four years," Fitzpatrick said. "Every guy brings something to the table. Obviously, some guys bring a lot more, like Johnny (Vanbiesbrouck) and Skrudland, but it's a total team effort. As long as we've got 20 guys pulling the rope, there is no reason for this team not to be successful."

Two nights later, the Panthers entertained the Rangers once again. And once again, the

interesting to have that challenge as a player or a coach. We matched up well against them, and that's what makes it exciting. Our guys match up with Gretzky, Messier, Leetch, Richter and Graves. It was a great game, to let them come back, and then finish them off was great."

A two-game road trip to Philadelphia and New York brought similar results to the season-

... most games at the beginning of the season without a loss.

"team" earned a victory. Six different Panthers scored, as Florida won, 6-4. The Panthers rushed out to a 5-2 lead before the Rangers cut it to 5-4. But Robert Svehla iced it with a goal in the final minutes.

"It is a situation where it is stars against a team," MacLean said. "It's really

opening trip. Lindsay scored the game-winner in Philly, as the Panthers continued their road mastery over the Flyers. Then Florida went into Madison Square Garden to play a hungry group of

Garpenlov (left) helped the Panthers win their first game in Denver, while Lindsay (above) continued his acrobatic goal-scoring. His game-winning goal helped the Cats past Philly.

GRIT and *Glory*

The Players

There's something about being told you're not wanted.

The very nature of an expansion draft provides motivation. When an expansion draft occurs, each team protects a certain number of players, thereby telling the rest of their team that they're not quite good enough, or not quite young enough, or not quite affordable enough to be kept.

The latter category probably is the easiest to accept, but nobody wants to have that word—exposed—attached to his name. It makes you feel so...exposed.

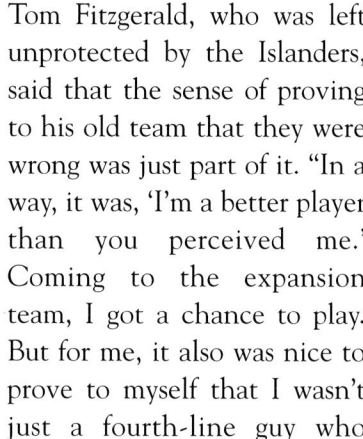

"Nobody likes to be told that they're not good enough to be protected in the top 15," Dave Lowry said. "I think it was a challenge for every guy the first year to prove that we still belonged in the league. There was a commitment that was given by the group the first year, the commitment to come every night and play hard and to work hard. We wanted to be part of something. We wanted to create an identity.

"If we weren't good enough to play on the other teams, we wanted to be known as a group of guys who were going to come here and were going to battle hard every night."

It may have helped a little bit that this was supposed to be the strongest expansion draft in league history. Each team was able to protect just one goalie, and 15 players over-

all, but still there was that stigma.

Each player came with a different story. Tom Fitzgerald, who was left unprotected by the Islanders, said that the sense of proving to his old team that they were wrong was just part of it. "In a way, it was, 'I'm a better player than you perceived me.' Coming to the expansion team, I got a chance to play. But for me, it also was nice to prove to myself that I wasn't just a fourth-line guy who could kill penalties, who got maybe two minutes a period. I got a chance to prove to myself that I could play."

John Vanbiesbrouck, the team's star goaltender who was able to soften the blow by being selected first overall in the expansion draft, said the proving is not directed necessarily at the players' old teams. "I don't think that we wanted to prove to the teams that let us go as much as we wanted to prove to each other that we could play, and we could play at a top level," he said. "We wanted to gain respect. It's no different from any other team at the start of the season every year. You've got to gain your respect every year."

When the Panthers made their selections in the draft, they looked for players they thought would take the motivation of not being protected and use it to play hard. It's the often-used term "character" that the

Panthers organization prides itself on. "They had a goal in mind to go a certain direction, maybe learning from the other expansion teams, that we need some character guys," Fitzgerald said. "Not that they weren't character guys on those teams, but maybe the teams were a little too young, and a little too inexperienced. (Former general manager) Bobby Clarke said from day one in the opening meeting in training camp, 'We're here to win. We're not here to be an expansion team. We're not here to take our lumps and win an occasional game. We're here to compete every night, and if we compete, we can win some games.'

"They drafted guys that they felt could fit."

Those guys jelled quickly. They knew that there were no superstars and that meant each man had to contribute for the team to be successful. One guy might score two goals on one night, but he wouldn't be counted on any more heavily than anyone else the next night.

"We have 20 players dress every night," backup goaltender Mark Fitzpatrick said. "That's how this team has been successful over the past four years. Every guy brings something to the table. Obviously, some guys bring a lot more to the table, but it's a total team effort. As long as we've got 20 guys pulling the rope, there is no reason for this team not to be successful."

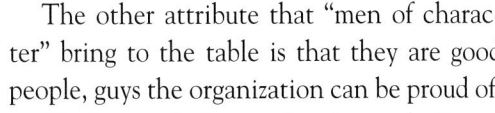

The other attribute that "men of character" bring to the table is that they are good people, guys the organization can be proud of.

Clarke, and former head coach Roger Neilson are two of the prominent men who helped put the team together. Although neither still is with the team, they agree that the nucleus of the team, those 10 players taken in the expansion draft who still wear the Panthers sweater, are quality people.

"I think we were fortunate that without knowing too many of the players personally, we ended up having good people and good families and the players were all low-maintenance type of players," Clarke said. "They were willing to work to sell the sport in the community, and they were not looking for anything out of it personally, other than helping sell hockey to that community. They would go out and do what was necessary, do it properly, and do it with decency and humility. That's fairly rare in professional sports now. Players, if they go out, want to be paid and want to be treated like superstars. These guys didn't."

Neilson added, "There have been many reporters I've known over the years from all the different teams I've been with, who would come up to me and say, 'That is the best bunch of guys.'"

The players have their priorities in

Fitzgerald (left, top), Lowry (left, bottom), Murphy (above, top), Fitzpatrick (above, bottom), Jovanovsky (next page, top) and Mellanby (next page, bottom) all are part of the big picutre.

order. On the ice, no team works harder. Off the ice, they fit into the community. It's why former public relations director Greg Bouris tabbed the Panthers "the franchise you can touch."

"I think that the reason why people want to reach out to us is that they feel that we have our priorities in order," Vanbiesbrouck said. "Not only can people say, 'See what this guy does, he scores a lot of goals, he stops a lot of pucks.' That stuff is on the perimeter. But they also can say, 'See Dave Lowry at school with his kids. He is a father first. And he's a hockey player second.'

"People like the hard work and lunch-pail-type crew that we are, and they know what they are going to get, and they're happy with it."

There really is no big piece to this puzzle. There are plenty of valuable, intricately interlocking pieces, each one necessary for the completion of the picture. Those pieces can be divided into three groups. Group 1 is made up of the wily veterans, those players like Vanbiesbrouck who were solid players with other teams who can provide leadership to the younger players. Group 2 is the younger veterans who were taken in the expansion draft or signed as free agents who have established themselves while with the Panthers.

The final group is made up of the new breed, the players who never saw the NHL in the PPE—the Pre-Panthers Era.

It's time for those guys to take control.

"In order for this team to get better, the younger guys really have to start stepping up their roles and stepping up their play," said Rob Niedermayer, the Panthers' first selection in their first NHL entry draft and one of the members of that category. "We know we're going to get a great effort from Brian Skrudland. We know we're going to get a great effort from Scott Mellanby. It's guys like Rhett Warrener, Ed Jovanovski, Radek Dvorak and me. Some of the young guys really have to step up their play in order for this team to keep getting better."

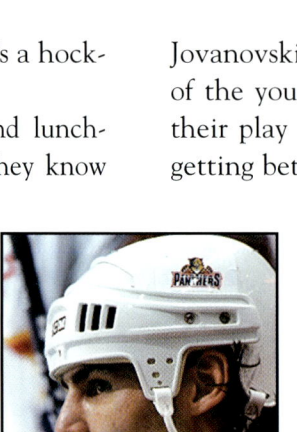

The outstanding expansion draft brought character and hard work. The entry drafts have brought talented young players. Key trades and free agent signings have filled holes. The Panthers made the Stanley Cup finals in their third year and reached the playoffs again in their fourth. Yet there still are skeptics. Some "experts" refuse to believe the Panthers are for real.

"A lot of the media keeps telling us we're no good, and the bubble is going to burst," Scott Mellanby said. "I think that kind of fuels our fire and creates a bit of a fear-factor. I think fear to a certain degree can be real good."

And to a certain degree, so can being told you're not wanted.

Rangers. Lowry scored for the Panthers, and the Beezer once again was stellar, letting in just one of New York's 35 shots in a 1-1 tie.

The Panthers stood 7-0-4 when they hosted the Chicago Blackhawks. The Hawks were one of two clubs (St. Louis was the other) that the Panthers had not beaten in their history. (They had not lost to Anaheim or Edmonton prior to the 1996-97 season. All four streaks were ended during the regular season.)

The game was knotted at 2-2 when Hough netted the game-winner at 17:43, and the Panthers stood a league best 8-0-4. That left them just three games short of tying the league's best start. If they could avoid losses in their next three games, they would match the Edmonton Oilers (12-0-3 in 1984-85) for the most games at the beginning of the season without a loss.

"We don't really talk about it," MacLean added, "It's not an issue. We know it's there, though. Everywhere we go now, teams are waiting to knock us off. It's really been a solid team effort. We have a lot of people playing so hard."

October ended perfectly for the Panthers. However, the streak had to end sometime—unless the Panthers were going to match the 1869 Cincinnati Redlegs (baseball) and the 1972 Miami Dolphins (football) as the only undefeated teams for an entire season in professional sports history—and that sometime came in their next game against Philadelphia.

The Flyers came to Miami Arena for a

Hough (above) and the Panthers seemed to be toying with the opposition early in the 1996-97 season. Hough scored the game-winner in the 12th game of the unbeaten streak.

contest on November 2. The start of the game was delayed for several minutes by a malfunction with the lights in the arena, but the Panthers could not delay the end of their streak. With just over a minute remaining, Joel Otto of the Flyers skated behind the net and stuffed the puck between Vanbiesbrouck and the post for the game-winning goal in a 3-2 loss. The Flyers tied the game with just over seven minutes remaining when Shjon Podein tipped in Eric Desjardins' miss.

... it's heartbreaking to lose a division game like this.

And while the Panthers seemed victimized by a blown call, the fact that Vanbiesbrouck faced 44 shots from Philadelphia (compared to 28 for Florida) revealed the real cause for the loss.

It was a disappointing end to the streak, but everyone knew that it had to end. "You know you're not going to go 82-0," Fitzgerald said, "but it's heartbreaking to lose a division game like this. We didn't play well and we didn't deserve to win."

The Panthers attempted to begin a new streak with a home game against Washington. Four different Panthers scored, Vanbiesbrouck stopped 24 shots and the Panthers once again were on the right side of the won-lost ledger, by a 4-2 margin. Another 4-2 win over Pittsburgh left the Panthers at 10-1-4.

A four-game stretch in which the Panthers went 1-2-1 dropped the Cats from the top spot in the league, but they kept the conference's best mark. But Murray was not satisfied with his team. Since the sweep by the Colorado Avalanche in the Stanley Cup Finals, Murray had insisted that the Panthers were too small in the middle. So on November 19, he pulled the trigger on a trade.

Murray sent fan favorite center Stu Barnes and defenseman Jason Woolley to Pittsburgh for 6-6 center Chris Wells. "We feel Chris gives us the size and strength we needed," Murray said. "(Stu) has been very good for the franchise, which made it more difficult for us to move him. But the next step was to try to get a bigger guy to play in the middle."

Wells got his first action as the Panthers hosted the Los Angeles Kings. He didn't score, in fact, he got his first goal as a Panther nearly three months later, but plenty of other Panthers did. The Cats dethroned the Kings, 4-1, beginning a four-game winning streak. A 2-1 win in overtime at Dallas (Jody Hull

With Niedermayer and Garpenlov on the bench with knee injuries, Carkner sitting with an ankle sprain, and Jovanovski watching because of a three-game suspension for leaving the penalty box early, the Panthers just relied on other players to carry the load. "That's pretty typical of a lot of our performances in the history of the team, not just now, but going back a few years," MacLean said. "They pride themselves in outworking teams. When you get a chance to coach a team like that, you're a pretty lucky guy.

"It's not just the guys who have been here three and four years. It's the Lindsays, the Lauses, the Strakas, the Fitzpatricks, a whole

scored the game-winner in the extra period) was followed by a 3-1 win in St. Louis. The Blues fans were hoping to see a goal by their own Hull (Brett), but again, it was the Panthers' Hull who scored the goal, this time putting the game away late in the third.

group of 24- to 27-year-olds, who are contributing. Then you've got five guys who are 19 to 21 who have picked up the work effort. That's a credit to the leaders."

 In an effort to get bigger in the middle, the Panthers pulled the trigger on a trade that sent Stu Barnes (left and above) and Jason Woolley to Pittsburgh for 6-6 center Chris Wells.

And while the Panthers had dispelled the idea that the 1995-96 version was no fluke, MacLean was not ready to label the 1996-97 team a repeat of the previous year. "I don't know if we can get too carried away," he said. "We're only 22 games in. We've got a long way to go. As everybody knows, there are so many factors that come into play. We're just trying to play consistent hockey. To this point I'm really happy. I've heard the word 'fluke' so many times that I don't know what it means any more."

I've heard the word 'fluke' so many times that I don't know what it means any more."

There was a lot of time left in the season, but with a little more than one-quarter of the season gone, the Panthers once again owned the best record in the league. They earned a win against Buffalo and a tie against Hartford at home, then traveled to Detroit and claimed a 4-2 win. A 1-1-1 stretch followed, before the Panthers embarked on an unbelievable road stretch.

From December 10 through January 23, the Panthers would play 15 of 19 games on the road. That would include stretches of eight of nine and 13 of 16. In one five-day stretch, the Panthers would play on the road at Ottawa, Chicago and both New York teams.

"It's the most ludicrous thing I've seen in a long time," MacLean said. "I've never experienced anything like this in 11 years, never heard of any team in this situation." Part of the problem was that the circus was booked in Miami Arena for the first two weeks of January, but MacLean was particularly incensed that the league forced his team to travel so much in late December when the arena was available.

"There's no explanation for it," he said.

The team began the odyssey with high expectations. Mellanby predicted a .500 record, adding "anything better would be great." But MacLean wanted no part of that number. "I thought we weren't going to mention .500 here anymore," he said. "That was a word we got away from a couple of years ago. I'm not going to be happy with .500."

Sheppard (left) got behind the Buffalo defense for his first hat trick in a Florida uniform. Jovanovski (above) often was a target for the opposition because of his physical style.

He should have been. When they left, they stood 17-5-7, the best record in the NHL. They also held a nine-point edge over Philadelphia in the Atlantic Division. But a 6-10-3 record during the 19-game excursion left them 23-14-10, which was fourth best in the league, third in the conference and second in the division. Although they managed to claim the conference's best

> **"After every game we lose my feeling is we'll win the next one."**

mark for a couple of days later in the season, they never held the league-best mark after the road marathon.

The first game was in Philadelphia, where the Panthers were 4-0-3 over the previous seven games. The Flyers scored twice in the first period and never looked back. They took leads of 4-1 and 5-2 before a couple of late goals made the 5-4 final score respectable for Florida.

Of course, the Flyers are among the elite in the NHL. A loss on the road, no matter how brutal, could be forgotten fairly quickly. But a 5-2 loss at Hartford, perennially one of the league's poorer teams, would be harder to understand. It produced the first two-game losing streak of the season. MacLean appeared unruffled.

"After every game we lose my feeling is we'll win the next one," he said. "I don't look any further than that. So I don't have a lot of concerns."

A 6-3 win over Edmonton, one of the few games at home, provided a reprieve, but that set up the six-game road trip that included the four games in five nights. Amazingly, the Panthers came through those four games with two wins (Chicago and the Islanders) and two losses (Ottawa and the Rangers). They stood 20-8-7, still the league's best record.

The Panthers got Garpenlov back from the knee injury in time for the game at Ottawa, and he scored one of two Florida goals when he lit the lamp in the third period. But four goals by Ottawa in the second period sealed the outcome. The loss at Ottawa dropped the Panthers' lead over Philadelphia in the Atlantic Division and the Eastern Conference to one point.

After the win in Chicago and the loss to the Rangers, the lead was zero. The two teams stood tied for the top spot. Since the All-Star Game coach was to be selected based on the conference leaders, it was time to look up the tie breakers. When deciding positioning for the post-season, the first tie breaker is wins. But in this case, the Panthers held a better winning percentage, because they had played two fewer games than Philadelphia, and MacLean was named to his second straight coaching honor.

"It's quite an honor, especially when the team

is in its fourth year in the league," he said. It's not like it's an award type of thing, though. I'm the one who reaps the benefits of a hard-working team and coaching staff."

The next night, the Panthers downed the Islanders when Ray Sheppard scored in overtime, and two straight ties at Tampa and

Bondra scored the tying goal with 8.4 seconds left in the third.

If the Panthers thought their break from the six-game stretch was going to be easy, they were wrong. The Canadiens closed the 1996 portion of Florida's schedule by claiming

Washington concluded the six-game trip. The tie at Washington was particularly tough to swallow. The Panthers held a 1-0 lead, thanks to Robert Svehla's first-period goal, in the final minute. But Peter

a 2-1 victory in Miami. It's tough to win when you score just one goal, but the Panthers tried to do something even tougher—win without

Garpenlov (left) came off his knee injury in time to score against Ottawa. A win over the Isles helped the Cats keep the best record in the East, earning MacLean an all-star berth.

scoring a goal—in their next game. The Anaheim Mighty Ducks, a team the Panthers had never lost to (3-0-1), came to Miami and shut out the Panthers, 3-0.

If the Panthers thought their break from the six-game stretch was going to be easy, however, they were wrong.

A five-game road trip followed the quick, two-game homestand. The Panthers opened it by slamming the Los Angeles Kings, 5-0. Niedermayer, who returned against Montreal after missing 17 games, opened the scoring in the first minute. Mellanby and Radek Dvorak added goals, and Murphy chipped in two.

Apparently, the Ducks liked this winning thing, though, because in the Panthers' next game, Anaheim won again, 3-2. The Ducks owned the first period. Warren Rychel, a player better known for taking penalties than scoring goals, got one past Vanbiesbrouck to give the Ducks a 3-0 lead with 2:02 left in the period. Lindsay cut the lead to 3-1 before the end

of the period, and David Nemirovsky added his first NHL goal, but Guy Hebert stopped all the Panthers' shots during the third period.

The Panthers' next game was at Calgary, Chris Wells' hometown. Wells had grown up close to the Olympic Saddledome, so the young center was psyched up. "The fact that the game is here makes it kind of a big deal," he said before the game. "I'm pretty nervous. I didn't sleep very well last night."

For once, it was hard to tell. Wells centered a line with Skrudland and Hull, and delivered some crunching checks in a 4-1 Florida victory. "He had a strong performance," MacLean said. "He did a great job on the wall and had three or four chances around the net that he just didn't get a handle on."

The Panthers traveled to Vancouver and couldn't get a handle on a victory, instead getting their league-leading 10th tie. Seven minutes into the third period, Fitzpatrick was run over by Scott Walker. Fitzy was motionless on the ice for several minutes and sustained a cut that took eight stitches. The Panthers chose

not to retaliate, fearing putting the Canucks' potent power play on the ice. But Alexander Mogilny ruined the plan, scoring on the first shot against Vanbiesbrouck.

The final game before the All-Star break saw the Panthers lose a 4-0 game at Edmonton. But it also saw the Panthers lose Jovanovski with a sprained right knee. JovoCop collided with Luke Richardson's knee at center ice. Richardson received a five-minute major penalty, but the loss was much greater for the Panthers. Jovanovski was expected to be out for four to six weeks.

"Eddie's a great young player," MacLean said. "It's a big loss for us. The one positive is we're pretty solid back there. We should be fine."

While MacLean, Vanbiesbrouck and Svehla traveled to San Jose for the All-Star Game, the rest of the Panthers returned home for a rest...and to prepare for the defending champion Colorado Avalanche. The last time the Avalanche were in Miami, they won the Stanley Cup with a 1-0 triple-overtime victory.

It wasn't as close this time, as Colorado rolled

to a 4-2 victory. The Panthers didn't have to worry about Patrick Roy this time, but Craig Billington stopped 33 of 35 shots.

The Panthers finally got to draw a conclusion to their 19-game marathon with games at Hartford and Boston. The game at Hartford had a stark contrast to an earlier game in Vancouver. When Keith Primeau poked his stick at Fitzpatrick after the goalie made a save in overtime, Fitzgerald and Hough went after him. What followed was a melee that would have made the WWF proud. Four game-misconduct penalties were called.

The Panthers lost Carkner and Svehla, and eventually lost the game when Robert Kron scored with just 13.8 seconds left. It was the Panthers' sixth loss in their last 11 games (2-6-3). They needed a tonic, and the Boston Bruins provided it.

The Bruins, who finished the season with the fewest points in the NHL, were gracious hosts. Dvorak got two goals, Sheppard added a goal and two assists, and the Beezer notched 28 saves as the Cats earned a 4-1 victory.

"This was a huge win for us," Niedermayer said. "We were in a bit of a slump, not getting too many breaks, and this really helps before going home."

The Panthers finally had an extended period at home, and they capitalized...at least until the Capitals came to town. The first of a four-game stretch brought the Lightning to Miami Arena, and the Panthers earned a 3-2 win. The Panthers were 0-3 on the power play, but all three chances were set up by Wells, who replaced an injured Skrudland (shoulder).

"I think Chris had a real good game," MacLean said.

The Ducks came to Miami and shut out Mellanby and the Panthers (left) to claim their first win in history over their fellow fourth-year team. Fitzgerald and the Panthers totally dominated the Canadiens when the came into town following the all-star break (above).

Mellanby broke out of a seven-game scoring slump by scoring two goals in a span of 50 seconds. Murphy, in his 600th career game, added the other goal. The Lightning outshot the Panthers 15-4 in the final period, but Vanbiesbrouck came up big. He then came up big in stature after the game as he confronted Alex Selivanov. The right winger had been harping at the Beezer all evening long—in Russian—and the Cats' goalie had had enough. Although there was just a little pushing, it made a point.

> "He was trying to get into my head. He can't even speak English."

"At the end of the game, I said 'Let's stop talking and do something about it,'" Vanbiesbrouck said. "He was trying to get into my head. He can't even speak English. I don't know what he was talking about."

The Canadiens were next on the schedule and they hardly made a dent. The Beezer stopped 30 shots and the Panthers won, 5-1. Boston followed the Habs and left with a 3-1 loss. It was the fourth straight victory for Florida.

The Panthers jumped out to a 3-0 lead midway through the second period, then tried to coast. Dvorak scored six minutes in and Svehla made it 2-0 less than three minutes later. Hull's goal made it 3-0. But the Bruins weren't out of it.

Ray Bourque took a pass from Adam Oates and scored to tie for Boston's all-time lead in points with 1:27 left in the second. The Bruins kept attacking the Florida zone, but Vanbiesbrouck stopped 18 shots in the third period alone to keep the Bruins from getting any closer.

"We played 20 minutes and John Vanbiesbrouck played 60," Sheppard said after the game.

The four-game streak matched the season's best, and Vanbiesbrouck was the big reason. He had not allowed a third-period goal, despite seeing 52 shots (compared to the Panthers' 31).

Washington was next on the schedule and they "tripped" the Panthers, 3-1. To be specific, Mike Eagles of the Caps knocked down Vanbiesbrouck behind the Panthers goal, and Anson Carter ripped a shot into the empty net.

"Ninety-nine out of 100 times they call that," Vanbiesbrouck said of the interference call that wasn't. "It's the first time I've (not) seen a call in that situation," added goaltenders coach Billy Smith, a Hall of Fame goaltender in his own right. The referee explained to MacLean that Eagles had tried to avoid the contact, but the goal—the Caps' second—put an end to the Panthers' streak.

The loss on the scoreboard was not nearly as costly as a loss during the game. Peter Bondra, an offensive threat for Washington not known for dirty play, collided knees with Sheppard midway through the second period. Sheppard was expected to miss several weeks with a sprain. It was the fourth significant knee injury—but not the last—that the team had suffered in the season. Garpenlov, Niedermayer and Jovanovski all had missed time from knee-to-knee collisions, and the loss of their top scorer in Sheppard would be tough to handle. What further exacerbated the Panthers' frustration was that Bondra was given just a one-game suspension.

"It was pretty blatant," Sheppard said. "Anybody who has seen the tape would say the same thing. If you use a knee, you have just as much chance of injuring yourself as somebody else. One game...that's ridiculous."

The games go on, however. A three-game road trip to Montreal, Buffalo and New Jersey saw the Panthers score just five goals. It also saw them give up five goals, All three games ended in ties, giving the Panthers a league high 13 ties through 54 games.

Garpenlov scored with three and a half min-

Wells (left) took awhile to get started once he arrived in Florida. But when Brian Skrudland went down, he stepped up and notched three assists versus Tampa Bay. Garpenlov may have lost this argument (above) but he got up in time to tie the score against Montreal.

utes remaining against Montreal to give Florida its first tie on the trip. Fitzpatrick stoned Brian Savage from the slot in the final minute of regulation, keeping the score knotted at 2-2.

The next stop was in Buffalo, and Skrudland made his return after missing five games with a strained shoulder. Lindsay scored the lone goal for Florida, and Fitzpatrick turned in his second straight strong effort, as the team's skated to a 1-1 tie.

Finally, in New Jersey, Garpenlov scored both goals for the Panthers and Vanbiesbrouck returned to the net with 33 saves in a 2-2 tie.

Mellanby took the first opportunity to go after Petit.

In his second game back after an injury, Skrudland fractured a rib and was expected to miss two or three more games.

The Panthers returned home to face the Rangers, the team just two points behind them in the Atlantic Division. If the Rangers stole a victory, the teams would be tied. And the Panthers were anything but full strength.

With Sheppard out, the role of leadership from the center position fell to Niedermayer. He responded favorably with a goal and an assist. He also held Messier without a point until late in the game.

The Panthers jumped out to a 3-1 lead after one period. Niedermayer opened the scoring with a power-play goal just 2:50 into the game. Vladimir Vorobiev answered on a Rangers power play just 1:12 later. Mellanby's 22nd of the year on a power play at 15:11 gave the Panthers the lead for good. Straka added the Panthers' third goal of the period at 17:31.

Hull made it 4-1 in the second period, and then the Rangers started their comeback. Sergei Nemchinov scored in the second and Adam

Graves scored in the third, but Vanbiesbrouck stopped 11 third-period shots (29 overall).

"With the injuries we have, and our kids playing, you've got to be very proud of them," MacLean said. The kids would become even more important, because the Panthers lost Dave Lowry with—you guessed it—a knee injury. He suffered a sprain of

the left medial collateral ligament. He was expected to miss seven to 10 days.

That meant the kiddie corps would be even more important as Tampa Bay came to town. Tampa Bay was in a battle for a playoff spot and needed points. But the kids came through. Nemirovsky tied the score after Dino Ciccarelli opened the scoring. Wells then scored the first goal of his Florida career before Ciccarelli tied it up. Svehla then scored and assisted on the Panthers' next two goals. Straka scored the fourth goal and then assisted Dvorak on the final goal, as the Cats won, 5-2.

The victory put the Panthers in first place in the Atlantic Division and the Eastern Conference. It was the first time in a month and a half that they occupied the top spot. Unfortunately, following a 1-0 overtime loss in their next game at the New York Islanders, they would drop out of the position and not see it again.

The loss to the Islanders was the first of three straight. Included in the skid was a 4-2 loss at Pittsburgh in which the Panthers saw their former teammate Stu Barnes for the first time. Barnes' trade in November had caused quite a stir, especially when he started hot and Wells, the player the Panthers acquired in the deal, didn't. While Barnes had enjoyed the ride in Pittsburgh, he felt compassion for Wells.

"I hear he's a nice kid with a good work ethic," Barnes said. "The game's tough enough without having to go through that. I hope things work out for him."

Of course, that sentiment was shared by the Panthers fans. Wells had been playing well in recent games, out of necessity. Hough returned to the lineup against Pittsburgh, but Sheppard, Jovanovski, Lowry and Skrudland watched the game from the press box.

The Devils were next, and they brought a 12-game unbeaten streak (6-0-6). The Panthers couldn't end it, but they did get one point in a 2-2 tie. Niedermayer and Lindsay scored for Florida and Fitzpatrick stopped 24 shots.

The Flyers followed the Devils and dealt the Panthers a couple of serious blows. Eric Lindros tapped in Eric Desjardins' shot with less than a minute remaining in overtime to give the Flyers a 4-3 victory. Worse than that, the Panthers lost Garpenlov to a knee injury when he collided knee-on-knee with Michel Petit. Like

the other casualties before him, Garpenlov was expected to be out for at least six weeks.

The Panthers had been criticized by the media and some fans for not retaliating in the past when one of their teammates had been hurt. Fitzpatrick and Vanbiesbrouck had been run over without any return attack. Rarely had an opponents' transgression been punished with a fist. The time had come.

Mellanby took the first opportunity to go after Petit. He started a fight that resulted in a two-minute penalty for instigating a fight, a five-minute major for fighting and a 10-minute

game misconduct. Petit got five minutes for fighting. The two-minute advantage for Philadelphia was fruitless, while the statement made by Mellanby said volumes.

With Sheppard out, the role of leader fell on Niedermayer (left), who responded with a goal and an assist in a 4-3 victory. Mellanby may not have liked sitting in the penalty box for most of a period, but he refused to ignore a knee-on-knee hit by Michel Petit on Garpenlov.

"I just felt because of what transpired earlier in the season somebody had to do it," Mellanby said. "Obviously, it's been made a real issue on our team."

The Panthers killed the penalty and even took a 2-1 lead on a shot by Jovanovski on his first game back from a knee injury. But the Flyers scored two more goals in the second period to take a 3-2 lead into the third. Jovanovski scored again in the third period to tie the score and the game went into overtime, where Lindros came up a hero.

The Panthers managed a tie against San Jose in its next game, followed by a win against St. Louis in overtime, the third straight game to go extra periods. Niedermayer had the game-winner in OT against the Blues, leading to a season sweep against a team the Panthers had not beaten before the season.

Coming off that high, the Panthers promptly went to Tampa Bay and got shut out (2-0), then returned home and tasted the same result against Phoenix (3-0). They had gone 1-6-2 in their last nine games, scoring a total of 14 goals. The slump left the Panthers in third place in the Atlantic Division, fourth in the conference and seventh in the league. They were spots they would hold the rest of the regular season. Two more losses, at home to Calgary and a depleted Boston, left the Panthers at a 29-23-15, the first time since they were 6-0-3 that they stood just six games better than .500.

"We have limited confidence around the net right now."

The first of those losses produced a loss that may have sealed the Panthers fate for the rest of the season. The Panthers' captain, Brian Skrudland, was lost for the season with a knee sprain. Although he was not the leader in scoring, his value to the team, especially in the playoffs, was immeasurable. He and Geoff Smith were the only players on the roster who had Stanley Cup rings.

I don't have to explain to anyone what Brian means to this franchise," Vanbiesbrouck said. "The players know it, the fans know it. It's why he wears the 'C.'"

The loss of Skrudland made a thin group of centers wafer-like. Once again the center position was being held down by youngsters, and this time there was no chance of a change without a trade. Most of the available centers had been dealt to other teams.

The 3-1 loss to Boston pointed out the problems the Panthers were having. Steve Washburn scored his first career goal, but nobody else added to their career totals. Fitzpatrick gave up two goals (the third was an empty-netter), running his total to just 14 in his last eight starts. That 1.75 goals against average translated to a 0-5-3 record. "We have limited confidence around the net right now," MacLean said, "and it's showing." Maybe losing to the Bruins, owners of the worst record in the league, woke up the Panthers. The Islanders came to town as Game 4 of a six-game homestand. It was exactly a month since their victory over Tampa Bay that gave them the conference's best record. That also was their last victory in regulation.

Mike Hough poked the puck out of the attempted grasp of Islanders goaltender Tommy Salo to give the Panthers a 3-1 lead with 3:39 remaining in the second period. The Islanders cut the lead to 3-2 in the third, but Vanbiesbrouck would not let any more pucks by him and the winless streak was history.

"Now that it's over, it's good that it was 3-2 because we showed good confidence the last eight minutes of the game," MacLean said. "We really didn't give them much."

The day after Skrudland underwent surgery to repair his knee, Vancouver arrived

Sheppard scored on his next two shots and the Panthers led, 5-2. Lonny Bohonos scored twice for Vancouver in the third, but the Beezer managed to stop just enough shots and the Cats won their second straight. The Panthers then tied Toronto and a once-horrid homestand finished with a three-game unbeaten streak.

Heading into New Jersey, the Panthers were mindful that their streak had not come against the league's top teams. Meanwhile, the Devils were as hot as anybody in the league. They had not lost a home game in 71 days. But the Panthers left the Meadowlands with a 4-1 victory. Lowry and Hull each scored his first goal in 15 games.

Bobby Holik actually scored the game-winner for Florida. Holik is a member of the Devils. Early in the third period, Holik tried to clear the puck to the corner, he accidentally slipped it behind the legs of his goaltender Mike Dunham. After a half-season of bad breaks, the Panthers were grateful for a good one.

"Those are the kinds of breaks we weren't getting during our losing streak," Lindsay said. "It's kind of nice to beat the hottest team in the NHL."

The Panthers had regained their form, but they still lacked the scoring punch they needed, especially with the injuries they suffered. They took a big step on the night of the trading deadline when they picked up center/left winger Kirk Muller in exchange for minor-league right winger Jason Podollan.

Muller was a 13-year NHL veteran. He had tallied 844 points in 952 games. As a member of the Montreal Canadiens in 1993, he had won a Stanley Cup ring. It was his experience that the Panthers

for a rematch of the "runover" game. Scott Walker had run over Fitzpatrick when the two teams played in Vancouver just before the All-Star Game, but no Panther had retaliated.

After a 5-4 victory, all the talk was centered on offense. Sheppard scored a hat trick—his third of the season—while Wells scored just his second goal of the season. But Wells' contribution may have been just as big as that of Sheppard. Sheppard got his first goal after Mellanby had given the Panthers a 1-0 lead in the first. But the Canucks got two goals in the final 3:59 of the first and the two teams headed for the locker room tied at 2-2.

Bret Hedican appeared to give Vancouver the lead early in the second period, but the toe of the skate of Martin Gelinas was in the crease, and the goal was disallowed. Sixteen seconds later, Wells beat Corey Hirsch when Hirsch tried to cut him off, then Wells hit the open net and the Panthers had a lead.

The Panthers still had some life left in them. They traveled into the Meadowlands and knocked down a Devils squad that had not lost at home in more than two months.

craved. "There were a variety of veteran players I talked about today," Murray said. "When it came right down to it, what he could bring to the table and the price involved, we felt he could bring to our team something that was sort of special."

Muller was not yet with the team as the Panthers traveled to Long Island for a seemingly winnable game against the Islanders. The Panthers scored four goals, but gave up seven. "A pathetic performance" was how MacLean described the game. The only bright spot was that the Rangers, the team in fifth place, five points behind the Panthers in the standings, also lost.

> ## "It seems the better the team, the better we play."

Muller joined the team in Ottawa on the following night, but the team performed in a similar fashion to the Islanders game. The Panthers trailed, 2-1, heading into the final period, but Hull got the puck past Damian Rhodes in the third to tie the score. While the Panthers could not grab another goal, their defense improved drastically in the third, holding Ottawa without a shot over a 10-minute stretch in the period.

Nine games remained and the Panthers held a six-point lead on the Rangers for the final home-ice spot in the playoffs. A three-game homestand was followed by a four-game road trip before the final two games of the season back at Miami Arena.

Buffalo was the first to arrive in town, and the Panthers outplayed the Sabres by much more than the 3-2 score would indicate. The Panthers did not allow a power-play goal in six Buffalo chances, including a four-minute advantage in the third. Offensively, the Panthers outshot the Sabres, 17-3, in the first period and totally dominated the game.

After Mellanby scored to give the Panthers a 1-0 lead—on an assist from Muller in his Miami Arena debut—the Sabres Miroslav Satan bedeviled Vanbiesbrouck to tie the score. Sheppard and Dvorak gave the Cats a 3-1 lead and a big enough cushion to withstand a late goal by Jay McKee.

"It seems the better the team, the better we play, which is a positive for us," Mellanby said. Of course, with Ottawa and Tampa Bay next on the list, maybe it wasn't a positive. Ottawa was a borderline playoff team and the Lightning were on the outside looking in. Murphy admitted that the players may be trying harder when the competition is keenest.

"Sometimes, though you don't want to admit it, you look at the other teams and say, 'They're below us, we should have this game,'" he said. "You don't ever go out with that mentality, but we've got to find a way to motivate ourselves the same way as we do for the top teams."

Ottawa came in five points out of the final playoff spot, so the Senators certainly

clinched a playoff berth, because Washington lost to Chicago, but the mood was far from jovial. "Making the playoffs around here is taken for granted," MacLean said, maybe forgetting that it was just the second berth in the four-year history of the franchise. Then he put it in perspective. "It's a big thing for a third- and fourth-year team (to make the playoffs two consecutive years)

had plenty to play for. However, a win and the Panthers were in the playoffs. While a berth was a foregone conclusion, it would be nice to make the invitation a formal one.

It was the Senators who got what they needed in the form of a 3-2 victory. The Senators jumped out to a 3-0 lead before the Panthers got two late goals.

The Panthers still

and I'll be shocked if it happens again."

The Panthers wanted to shock people by getting their offense going again as Tampa Bay ventured down the state. It did, but almost too late. The Lightning scored a short-handed goal, the fifth the Panthers

The addition of Muller (left) gave the Panthers the experience and goal-scoring they craved. Nemirovsky (above) and the Cats could not hook the big win they needed against Ottawa.

had given up in the last five games compared to just two power-play goals scored in the same period. With the final minutes of the third period ticking down, the lone goal was standing up. But Fitzgerald was able to shake free of Roman Hamrlik in the slot and fired the game-tying goal with less than two minutes remaining.

It wasn't a win, but it wasn't the loss that nearly happened either. "We're up five points with six games left," MacLean said. "Every point is critical."

Three games later, the Panthers still were looking for their next point. Losses at Pittsburgh (4-3), Toronto (3-1) and Boston (4-2) had the Panthers clinging to a one-point lead for fourth place. A 3-3 tie at Washington left them with two opportunities to claim home-ice advantage in the first round of the playoffs.

Of course, in 1996, they waited until the last game of the season to do so. Kind of like sliding under the gate of the store in the mall on Christmas Eve. They had their last two games at home, against New Jersey and Pittsburgh, and this time they did their shopping on the 23rd.

The Panthers fell behind the Devils, 1-0, when Jay Pandolfo got the puck past Vanbiesbrouck at the 13:35 mark. The Panthers had been 0-19-7 when they trailed entering the third period. But Niedermayer tied the score 4:44 into the period. Lowry scored the first of his two 1:21 later and the Panthers had a lead they would not relinquish.

Lowry also netted the Panthers' third goal at 13:25. New Jersey's Bobby Holik cut the lead to 3-2 on a power play. But the Devils could not get past the Beezer, and when Dvorak scored an empty-netter with 37 seconds remaining, the Panthers had sewn up the

fourth spot in the Eastern Conference for the second straight year.

It really was an unlikely victory, looking at it on paper. Not only did the Panthers overcome a third period deficit, they ended a six-game winless streak (0-4-2) while stopping the Devils' six-game unbeaten streak.

The final game, now just a tune-up for the playoffs, saw the Panthers win by the same 4-2 score, but it was a different game than the previous one. Niedermayer scored first for Florida just 25 seconds into the game. Petr Nedved tied it midway through the period, but Sheppard scored in the second and Muller scored on the power play 2:05 into the third to give Florida a two-goal cushion.

For the second straight year, the regular season was just the preliminary.

Lemieux scored on a penalty shot, but Vanbiesbrouck stopped all 14 shots taken during game action and the Panthers hit an empty net again (Hull) for the final margin.

The Panthers finished the season 35-28-19, good for 89 points. The 19 ties were a league high. The 89 points were three fewer than in 1995-96, when they finished 41-31-10. And after going the first 12 games of the season without a loss, it was a letdown.

Blame it on the knees. Blame it on the fact that other teams were gunning for the defending conference champions. Blame it on the fact that the Panthers still lacked a 50-goal scorer. Blame it on...whatever you want. It didn't matter now. The Panthers were in the second season, where they would host the New York Rangers.

For the second straight year, the regular season was just the preliminary.

The Panthers still have not had a 50-goal scorer in their history, but a healthy Sheppard (left) could be that player. He was one of several players to miss games with knee injuries.

The Panthers opened the 1997 playoffs in very similar circumstances as they had in 1996. They were the fourth seed in the Eastern Conference, and as such got to open the playoffs at home. But they had limped home in the last part of the season. They had fallen from the top spot in the East as late as February 12, to fourth, barely maintaining the home-ice advantage.

And they were playing a team with far more playoff tradition, in this case the New York Rangers. The Blue Shirts didn't just bring the bright lights of New York, however. They also had a roster full of Stanley Cup heroes. Wayne Gretzky, the all-time leading scorer in NHL history as well as the all-time leader in playoff goals and assists, was making his Rangers playoff debut. Mark Messier, who had teamed with Gretzky for four of the Edmonton Oilers's five Stanley Cups in the mid- to late-1980s, had helped the Rangers erase a 54-year splotch on their record when he led them to the Cup in 1994. Add Mike Richter, Brian Leetch, Adam Graves, Glenn Healy, Jeff Beukeboom and Esa Tikkanen to the list, and the Rangers were loaded.

Of course, for the Panthers' John Vanbiesbrouck, a former Ranger, any contest against his old team was special. The fact that it was in the playoffs made it even more so.

But if Vanbiesbrouck had extra butterflies, it was hard to tell. The Beezer was nothing short of spectacular in Game 1. He stopped 34 New York shots as the Panthers won, 3-0. After a scoreless first period, Johan Garpenlov slipped the goal past Richter at 6:06 of the second to give Florida a 1-0 lead. Kirk Muller scored his first playoff goal for the Panthers at the 13:13 mark of the second, and just 1:54 later, Rob Niedermayer made it 3-0.

It was the fourth career playoff shutout for Vanbiesbrouck.

Special teams were key for both teams. The Panthers, who had finished the regular season ranked 21st in the league in power-play conversions, scored two of their three goals with a man advantage. Meanwhile, the Rangers, who had led the league in the same category, went scoreless in five attempts. In the first period, the Rangers had eight shots on goal during a penalty to Paul Laus, but could not get the puck in the net.

In the second period, they could fare no better when Garpenlov was assessed a penalty. But the Rangers' third period opportunity was the most telling. Niedermayer picked up a roughing penalty and 15 seconds later, Billy Lindsay was called for high sticking. For the next 1:45, the Rangers had a five-on-three advantage but could not touch the net. In fact, they only got one shot, and the Beezer handled it easily.

"If anything, it was just overpassing," Gretzky said of his team's inability to score. "They did a nice job (on defense), and when they broke down, Vanbiesbrouck made some nice saves."

The Panthers had a 1-0 lead, and had history on their side. In their brief playoff history, they had won each of the three series in which they had won the first game.

Exit from Eden

 The 1997 post-season did not end as the Panthers and their fans expected. A first-round series loss to the New York Rangers sent the Cats on a summer vacation a couple of months early. But it didn't dim the enthusiasm for this team, nor the expectations for the coming seasons.

But the Rangers turned the tables in Game 2, winning by the same 3-0 score. This time it was Richter pitching the shutout, his seventh in his post-season career. The Panthers were the ones with the shot advantage (11-4 in the first 12 minutes, compared to the Rangers' 10-1 lead in Game 1), and the Cats also were the team to blow a five-on-three chance in the third. For the Rangers, a familiar source got them rolling.

"I looked at it go through my legs."

Panthers' unfulfilling attempt at a five-on-three in the third, Luc Robitaille finished the scoring 3:29 in on an assist from Gretzky.

The teams headed for New York tied at a game apiece, but when Game 3 was done, the Panthers and Coach Doug MacLean were fit to be tied. The Panthers lost, 4-3 in overtime, but not before they endured a couple of controversial calls.

The Panthers fell behind early when Mike Eastwood scored on a rebound at 13:12 of the first. Ed Jovanovski gave up the puck in his

Gretzky opened the scoring at the 13:15 mark, beating Vanbiesbrouck in the five hole. "Did I get a good look at it?" Vanbiesbrouck asked rhetorically. "Yeah, I looked at it go through my legs."

Less than two minutes after Gretzky scored, Messier broke through the Panthers' defense and fed Graves, who set up Tikkanen. The second goal came on a power play just like the Panthers' did in Game 1. Following the

own zone and Doug Lidster fired a shot from the point. The rebound came to Niklas Sundstrom, who attempted the put it past Vanbiesbrouck. When his shot rebounded to Eastwood, the Rangers owned a 1-0 lead.

Robitaille increased the lead with his second goal of the playoffs after knocking the puck loose from Jovanovski. Eastwood gained control and fed Robitaille for a one-timer, and the Rangers held a 2-0 lead at the first intermission.

But the Panthers came out hot in the second. Garpenlov netted his second goal of the playoffs on the power play at 1:16. Ray Sheppard added a goal at 2:58, and the Panthers had tied the game within the first three minutes of the second period. When

and added an extra skater. They kept pounding the puck in on Vanbiesbrouck, and finally, with less than 19 seconds remaining, Robitaille corraled the loose puck to the Beezer's right and poked it back in, sending the game into overtime.

Robert Svehla scored on another power play at 15:32, the Panthers had the lead and control of the hockey game.

It stayed that way until the final seconds ticked down. The Rangers pulled Richter

The Panthers got the first big chance in overtime. In fact, they got the first goal. It just didn't count. Garpenlov fired a shot from the

The Rangers and the Panthers did hold anything back in their playoff series. Just ask Robert Svehla and Mark Messier (left). David Nemirovsky (above) showed why Panthers fans have high hopes for the future as he split a triple team of Rangers players in Game 5.

right wing that deflected off Leetch's skate and got past Richter, but Dan Marouelli waved off the goal saying that Scott Mellanby had interfered with Richter in front of the net. MacLean did not agree. He argued the call to no avail, but General Manager Bryan Murray was still hot after the game.

... this was the first time they faced elimination this early.

"Richter plays two feet out of his net on the play," he said. "He runs into his own player and Leetch kicks it in—it's a goal. Of course (Mellanby pushed Leetch into Richter), Mellanby was driving for the front of the net. But the goaltender, when he gets out of the net, can't block you from getting to the front of the net just because he has pads."

More than a month after the game, President and Governor Bill Torrey still felt the call, "could have turned the whole series."

Not only did the game-winning goal not count, but the Panthers were forced to kill another penalty. The Rangers did not score on the power play, but skating a man down is tiring enough without the added pressure of overtime in the playoffs.

Finally, at 16:29 of the first overtime period, Tikkanen fired a shot from the right point. It beat Vanbiesbrouck top shelf, but clanged—or so the officials thought—off the cross bar. The sound they heard was the puck hitting the goal camera and caroming out.

Play continued, but at the next whistle, the play was reviewed. "The guys upstairs screamed 'That's a goal!'" Tikkanen said. "I don't know what took so long to announce it." After several minutes, the official announcement gave Tikkanen the goal and the Rangers the victory.

The Panthers had a chance to come right back and regain the momentum as the two teams faced off the next night in Madison Square Garden. The Knicks' NBA playoff series had the preference of dates, and the Knicks were slated to open their series against the Charlotte Hornets the following night.

The Panthers got on the board first, scoring on a power play at 13:23.

The Gretzkys, er, the Rangers, tied the score in the second when "The Great One" took a feed from Leetch on a power play and got it past Vanbiesbrouck. Before the second period was done, Gretzky had scored two more goals and the Rangers held a 3-1 lead heading into the final period.

David Nemirovsky scored his first career playoff goal just 1:40 into the period, and the Panthers were back in the game. Nemirovsky was 3 years old when Gretzky broke into the league in 1979, and he could only relish scoring in the same game as his hero. "Me and a lot of kids grew up idolizing Gretzky," he said. "He's Wayne Gretzky.

That's all you have to say."

Unfortunately, Richter was heroic as well. The Panthers could not connect on nine more shots in the period, and the Rangers owned a 3-1 lead in the series.

"It's been 19 years of this," MacLean said of Gretzky's efforts. "That's why he's the greatest player to ever play the game."

The Panthers were in dangerous territory. They were one loss away from calling for tee times. They stood 2-1 in elimination games in their history. They beat Pittsburgh twice the

this series as favorites, another new experience, and they needed a win at home to get things rolling again.

History was not on their side, either. No team since 1984 had returned to the Stanley Cup Finals the year after losing in the championship series. The Panthers' own history was not much better. After the Game 4 loss, they stood 0-10-1 in games in which Lindsay did not play. Lindsay would be out of action for Game 5, as was Garpenlov. And of course, Brian Skrudland still was out.

previous year after the Penguins took a 3-2 series lead in the conference finals. Down 3-0 to the Avalanche in the Stanley Cup Finals, they lost the triple-overtime 1-0 thriller.

But this was the first time they faced elimination this early. The previous year they had defeated the Bruins four games to one and downed the Flyers in six games. They had entered

"They're missing some key players," Rangers coach Colin Campbell said. "Lindsay's a big key for them, as is Skrudland. When you get in one-goal and overtime games, that makes a huge difference."

MacLean had told ESPN that he was confi-

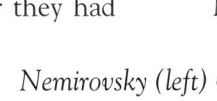

Nemirovsky (left) was 3 years old when Wayne Gretzky debuted in the NHL and he could only marvel as his idol scored all three goals in the Rangers' Game 4 victory. Messier (above) was held without a goal in the series until he broke through in Game 5 with two.

dent that his team could win the series if it just got to Game 5. One of the areas in which it had done a good job was defensing the Rangers' best line. Through four games, Messier, the second-leading scorer in playoff history (behind Gretzky), both in terms of goals and assists, had not lit the lamp even once. But while the Panthers needed a quick start to grab back the

With just 15 seconds left in the period, the Rangers once again took the wind out of the Miami Arena.

momentum, Messier had a personal hurdle to clear.

Thirty-nine seconds into the game, Messier cleared that hurdle with ease. He slipped behind the defense and took a perfect feed from Leetch. He faked left and then went right and snuck one between Vanbiesbrouck's legs for a 1-0 Rangers lead. The momentum the Panthers needed was firmly seated on the New York bench.

The Panthers did not give up. They outshot the Rangers, 9-7, and held the puck in the Rangers' end for much of the action. At 14:17 of the first period, Mike Hough ripped a shot past a fallen Ulf Samuelsson and tied the score at 1-1.

Florida dominated the second period, continually throwing the puck in at Richter's feet, but the Rangers' keeper kept covering up. As the clock ticked down the final seconds of the second period, Samuelsson picked up a loose puck in the neutral zone. He crossed the blue line on the right side and watched Messier reach the offensive zone to his left. Samuelsson fed the puck to Messier as he came to the middle. Messier then let one fire. It hit the stick of a defenseman and rose faster than the Beezer expected. With just 15 seconds left in the period, the Rangers once again took the wind out of the Miami Arena and went to the locker room with a firm hold on the momentum.

The third period saw the Panthers raise their aggressiveness another step. They controlled the puck, but had no luck getting a goal. They killed a couple of penalties, a key since the Rangers were the league's best power-play team during the regular season, but they also blew another one of their own.

Finally, with 7:42 remaining in the third, Tikkanen picked up a penalty after taking down Muller in front of the Rangers net, and the Panthers finally capitalized. Sheppard fired a shot from the left wing that hit off the skate of Brian Leetch in front of the net.

The game now seemed ready for the Panthers to grab hold. The crowd was going crazy. The Rangers, who use three lines most of the time, was a team of older veterans, whom one could guess would be tired.

But the Panthers could not get that last goal that would give them the lead and probably the game. As the final seconds of the third period ticked away, the two teams headed to overtime.

The Panthers also had the first opportunity to put the game away in overtime. Samuelsson was given a penalty for holding Mike Hough, but the Panthers never got off a serious shot.

Messier finished his miraculous night by setting up Tikkanen for the game-winner. Messier charged down the ice apparently headed for a

The intensity (and the beard) on Dave Lowry's (left) face showed that the playoffs had arrived. Niedermayer (above) is now a grizzled veteran of four seasons with the Panthers. He represents the present, and the future of this young franchise with high hopes ahead.